THE JANITOR'S CLOSET

or

How to Get into the Cleaning Business
and Stay There!

Richard C. Meehan, Jr.

The Janitor's Closet

or

How to Get into the Cleaning Business and Stay There!

by

Richard C. Meehan, Jr.

Noggin Universe Press

Printed in the United States of America
First Printing: April 2016

ISBN-10: 1530764351
ISBN-13: 978-1530764358

Richard C. Meehan, Jr.

TABLE OF CONTENTS

DEDICATION

To Pop – you always reminded me by your words and actions to never give up.
To Mother – your courage despite the odds of success have been an inspiration.
To my wife and children – thanks for putting up with my literary indulgences.
To Gail McAbee and my writing friends – your passion is infectious!

Richard C. Meehan, Jr.

FOREWORD

The material you are about to read comes from firsthand knowledge of the cleaning industry gathered by me, myself, and I, Richard C. Meehan, Jr., the S.O.B. (son-of-boss) at Marko, Inc., supplier of janitorial and cleaning products to the Upstate of South Carolina. My father started me off right in nineteen sixty-eight, mowing the grass with a sling blade in the front yard of the rented warehouse he used for his business. Upon the first stroke of the blade I nicked my leg and drew blood. Upon the second stroke, I beaded sweat. After all, it was summertime when school was out. Upon the third stoke, I choked back tears because I had a long way to go. I was eight years old, learning the work ethic of my parents: hard work has its rewards. Now I can speak intelligently on a variety of subjects about the cleaning industry, especially sanitation.

Sanitation…now there's a word I haven't actually used myself in years, although our corporate motto is "Health through…Sanitation…through Chemistry." Times change; styles change. Back in the day, when Marko was a fresh upstart competing with established supply houses, the "huckster" style of selling called for the use of that word. A huckster was a salesman who peddled goods with a pushy, haggling, no-nonsense manner. Our salesmen brandished the terms "sanitation," "janitorial," "chemical," and "disinfectant" at unsuspecting clients who were seeking products that actually did what the labels claimed, in other words, worked.

Some things never change, except perhaps the number of garage chemists mixing soaps to sell to janitors as "the latest, greatest, safest cleaner on the planet!" Years ago, before they became an endangered species, I actually witnessed one of these mix masters drink his concoction to prove how safe it was. The terminology "gastrointestinal distress" sprang to mind as I watched the demonstration. He must have been a real life iron man though, because he made it back to his car before any mishap. Thus, I began to understand that the World of Clean is not for the faint of heart.

Merriam-Webster's dictionary says that sanitation is "the promotion of hygiene and prevention of disease by maintenance of sanitary conditions." So what does "sanitary" mean? Using the same dictionary: "of or relating to health, characterized by or readily kept in cleanliness." A good word, sanitation: it kind of covers it all don't you think? Keeping things clean to promote health. That's the cleaning industry in a nutshell.

This sounds so easy, doesn't it? Keeping things clean and sanitized? As I grew, my father was careful to insure that I continued to have challenges related to the family business. I was a part of it; it was a part of me. Once I was big enough to sling a mop, the summer job changed to working in the newly formed Briter Business Service Division. Office cleaning, brick cleaning, stripping and waxing floors, glass cleaning – I learned about the true nature of the World of Clean. It was tough, but rewarding. I think I got paid anyway.

Before we go much further, perhaps I should mention a few conventions I will use in this book. The cleaning industry is so broad that you may catch me describing it in different terms. For instance, the World of Cleaning, Industry of Clean, cleaning industry, janitorial business, maid service, contract cleaning service, janitorial contractor, janitorial business, janitorial and cleaning business, jan/san, janitorial service, and other variations will be used to describe those who use elbow grease to scrub, strip, disinfect, deodorize, restore, polish, maintain, clean, sanitize, degrease, and in general, keep our lives safer by killing germs and removing detritus. No matter how you cut it or how you call it, the World of Clean is very much a hands-on trade.

Much janitorial work occurs after normal business hours. There's no way around it. After all, how can you mop a hallway if people are just going to keep tracking across those freshly cleaned floors? How can you strip wax and reapply a couple of fresh coats if people are just going to muck through it after you leave? How can you clean a restroom to make it fresh for the next day if you are shoved out of the way by needy personnel that don't want to visit the other restroom two halls down? What should you do if a client loses the money in their desk drawer and accuses you of taking it? How do you handle the irate customer that says her desk phone still has dust on it after you stayed all night detailing her cluttered office just to keep her happy so you don't lose the contract? These and many other interesting questions will be answered in this book.

As I continued to grow, becoming a strapping young man, so did the weight of the burdens I carried. There's nothing like packaging hundreds of pails of pine oil disinfectant in a stifling hot mixing facility housed under a tin roof with four other sweaty guys every day for weeks to fill contracted orders from the State. Pine oil lends such a fresh, clean smell to a building when used by the maid in the mop water. Bah, humbug! The scent of pine could not be removed from clothes, hair, skin, shoes, or anything else. All I can say is my friends thought I was mighty high-smelling when I'd come around after work. However, my wife-to-be thought I just naturally exuded a weird odor, something I found out about years after we were married. Now that's Love. I'm glad my father, the chemist, eventually developed other scents like Spring Breeze, Lemon Fresh, and Cheery Cherry. Just the thought of pine scent impels me the other way these days.

Then came the driver's license – yes, I got one. Deliveries to the janitorial staff of many companies all over the town of Spartanburg, South Carolina, in an ancient turquois Chevy pickup truck became my new task. I got to know the people behind the scene of Clean. Many different folks, male and female, black and white, green and purple – you name it – found employment by doing the dirty work most people will not do. After all, who wants to clean up behind others? It takes a special person to do that, or so I was told.

On a particular delivery to one of the local jailhouses I discovered that even inmates got the opportunity to enjoy the fun of cleaning. I watched two of them play bumper cars with rotary floor scrubbing machines, while two more of their buddies rode the machines like maniacs. It was especially entertaining when the machines collided and one of the inmates was ejected from his perch. Money changed hands around the spectators. What fun can be had while buffing the floors to a shine! What a shame that other companies needed cleaning supply deliveries that day. The jailhouse was air conditioned. And, we got to repair the broken machines the next day – for a price, of course.

Eventually I graduated from Wofford College in nineteen eight-two, right here in Spartanburg. During those days I juggled classes and part time work at Marko. I had learned to type and do mathematics in high school, so I became a great asset to my mother, the company secretary. The sextuplicate invoices had my name written all over them. Have you ever made a typographical error using a manual Royal typewriter on a sextuplicate form? Everyone should try it. There's nothing like slipping the form out of the machine, using an ink eraser pencil to rub out the mistake on six copies without tearing the thin paper, and then try to line that form back up exactly where you were before you took it out. Heavenly, I'm here to tell you. Or, how about running a manual adding machine with the crank on the side to calculate a huge column of figures that should balance with the bank statement when done, yet was always a few pennies off? Nothing to it! Graduation from college came along with these words: "Son, I had a salesman quit on me yesterday, so you'll take his place on Monday morning, eight A.M sharp! Dress in your Sunday best and don't be late!" So much for the summer off to travel around the country on money I had saved for years as my graduation reward to myself.

Selling janitorial supplies is an experience, not a job. This is where my education really began. Forget about having lived and breathed the cleaning industry since I was a kid, especially over the supper table. Anyone who has ever been a maid or janitor knows more about cleaning than anyone who grew up in the industry. In fact, these people know just about everything, so why have I even bothered to write this book? Yes, I'm being facetious, but only because so many of us forget to listen when others are trying to help. Or, maybe it's because of the question I get multiple times every week: "What will it cost for me to get into the cleaning business?" This is a pithy question that goes far beyond mere monetary value, although a number figure is what is expected. If you really want to know the true costs of running your own cleaning service, read on. Keep in mind that selling your services is a major part of owning your own business, so a good dose of sales techniques is coming your   way   too…

Richard C. Meehan, Jr.

GETTING INTO THE BIZ

Almost daily I meet new hopefuls excited about the prospect of "going into the business." Usually these folks have worked for cleaning contractors or have been on the janitorial staff at some large company, school, hospital, church, or municipality. They come into the showroom to determine if we sell the products they need. A glance at all of the equipment and supplies is enough to answer that in a positive way. Their attention then swings onto me with the usual comment, "I'm (We're) thinking of going into the cleaning business." After a few pleasantries, the Number One Question springs forth, "How much will it cost?" In reality, all it takes is a few thousand bucks, a handful of clients, and voila! You're in the cleaning business! How long you last in the business is another story.

If I were to put a figure, based on my company's sales data, to the number of startups that make it through the first six months, it would be somewhere around one out of ten; those who make it past the first year, maybe one out of twenty-five. Veterans of the cleaning industry, the ones who make it past twenty years, are so rare you'd think they were Bengal tigers. They are the ones who can afford an actual Yellow Pages ad, not just a highlighted text listing. Bengals command respect for their achievements. Although endangered by environmental conditions; i.e., the economic climate, they certainly must know the secrets of staying in business. These tigers must be doing a few things right, and I happen to know what those things are.

Before I divulge that information, you must ask yourself, "Am I ready to take on the responsibilities involved with opening my own cleaning service?" Now, before you jump out with your answer, keep reading to see how the Bengal tigers survive. Only then will your answer eventually make you a survivor too. I should at this point mention that I am not addressing how to start a franchise here, although you can take your company as far as you wish. No, I am discussing what a startup cleaning company can do to stay in business longer than it takes to wear out their first vacuum cleaner and make a profit in the meanwhile.

Bengal tigers face threats in the form of habitat loss and poaching. In economic terms, habitat loss comes from a flood of folks trying to open new cleaning companies in your area. This leads to markets that are glutted with competitors, which in turn leads to poaching in another's territory. Unfortunately, the current job market is rather skimpy right now; there's not enough meat to go around. Many people have been out of work for a while, most unwillingly. They are capable of doing something to make a living, but what? Light bulb flash – let's go clean stuff! Even if you clean something really well, that doesn't set you apart from the next company to come along with a lower price. There must be other assets that the tigers have than simply a bunch of stamina.

The World of Clean, like the Natural World, runs by Darwinian Theory. Charles Darwin postulated that only the strong survive – survival of the fittest. I prefer to think of this as an overall package – a bundle of traits gathered through experience within the marketplace. The Bengals have obtained these traits already. You will need them too if you plan to survive.

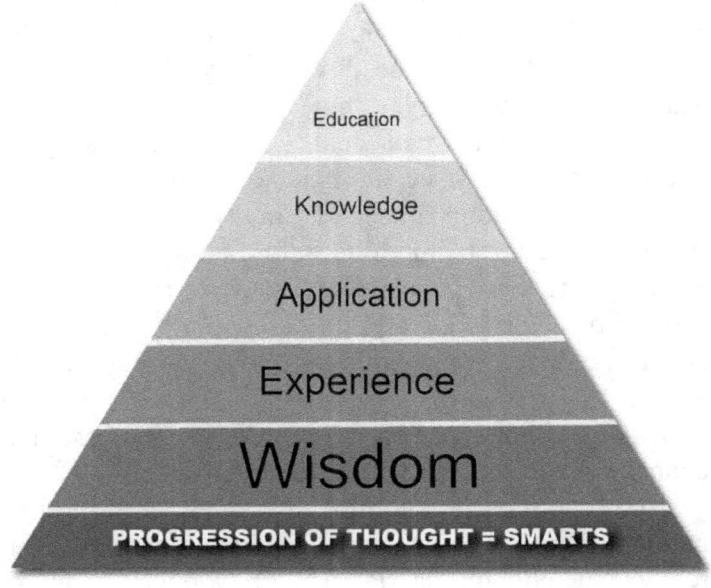

In simpler terms we call these traits "smarts."

Smarts, that's what the tigers have. They take their time; build their territory; learn the ins and outs of the cleaning industry like the back of their paws. They know there is more to it all than simply licking fur better than everyone else. Through patience they gain wisdom until they can drive competitors away from their meat. Smarts has to be earned; it is a progression of thought. With education comes knowledge, with knowledge comes application, with application comes experience, and with experience comes wisdom.

Your next question should be, "How can I get some?" "Therein lies the rub," to quote Shakespeare's Hamlet. Unfortunately, the attitudes of most of the folks I meet who want to get into the business already know everything. They've been there, done that. Stripped floors? Oh, yeah, many times. Applied the latest acrylic floor finishes? Absolutely, like glass too. Maybe they have, maybe they haven't. I usually find out soon enough when next I get, "Your stripper doesn't work!" or "The floors look dull and hazy after we used your floor finish!" In my line of work, the products take the blame long before admission of user error, if ever. Few people will fess up to not following instructions. Instead, I end up defending my products, and my advice, mainly due to the prevailing attitude within the trade. This is why I harp on gaining knowledge and experience in order to increase the chances of success – smarts – not smarty pants!

To run a cleaning company, it takes far more than manual labor done properly. Although no one can really get enough schooling, Knowledge is about information and wisdom – "smarts" is my colloquial description. Since the cleaning trade is a manual field, anything that makes it more rewarding is a good thing. Obviously moneymaking is what the trade is all about. So how do you turn a higher profit? Are you afraid I'm getting ready to say "crack the books?"

It is simply not enough to ask, "What will it cost for me to go into the business?" If this is your only question, think again. There is much more to running a cleaning service than simply making things clean. Believe me, as a person whose very survival depends on selling cleaning products to the sanitation industry I am always excited to help a new business get started. Unfortunately, most of these new businesses close in a few months simply because the whole picture of the World of Clean is ignored. It is with heavy heart that I say this because I need their continued business through regular purchases of cleaning supplies.

As a chip off the old block, when I want something to happen, I make it happen, for good or ill. Some people call this being stubborn. I call it the entrepreneurial spirit. This spirit is also one incorporating an informed decision. Informed decisions are made based on *information*. Entrepreneurs may try and fail despite using the knowledge they gain, but at least they go in with their eyes open. A failed situation perhaps, yet I give respect for the due diligence; whereas the quickest way to commit business suicide is to ignore the volumes of information at your disposal that would induce a better chance at survival. Nearly always, despite my recommendations concerning equipment, products, and especially book learning, new cleaning agencies go forward on a shoestring and a prayer. That's their prerogative, even if it means they close within the first six months. Tigers prowl around gathering data on their environment so they can find meat. I advise the same; otherwise, your belly will be empty.

Yes, I tend to harp on acquiring more knowledge to increase profits. Although it has a wonderful sound – p...r...o...f...i...t...s – many business wannabees simply do not understand what I'm driving at. Let's face it, the cleaning industry as a whole has a reputation for employing educationally challenged personnel. Many owners barely made it through high

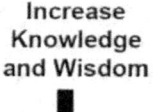

school, much less college. Few janitors and maids reached beyond high school. None of this really matters in the World of Clean, especially if you understand that this industry is as much a trade as bricklaying or carpentry. A good cleaning person learns tricks of the trade from someone with more experience. It may not take a lot of studying to sling a mop or scrub with a brush, but a true professional can make a facility look so good that it sings without a diploma. Unfortunately, to run a cleaning business it takes far more than manual labor done properly. Although no one can really get enough schooling, knowledge is not simply about books. Knowledge is about information and wisdom. Of course, what any good business owner wants is to take more money to the bank. If some of that money gets to stay there instead of being spent on the costs of doing business, that's really great. This excess is called Profit.

STALKING YOUR QUARRY

Not long ago I spoke with a husband and wife after regular business hours in my showroom about "going into the business." This is a common occurrence at my place. Excited, the prospective new cleaning team asked the Number One Question within moments of arrival in hopes of getting an idea of what it might cost for them to get started. As you have gathered, this approach to opening a cleaning service is a method I wholly discourage. So, without popping their balloon, I presented an idea used by the tigers – stalk your quarry. Learn their ways. Find their weaknesses. Pounce on opportunities. If opportunities don't present themselves, make them instead. The quarry is of course those potential customers gathered around the water source, or the "customer pool."

Another way to look at the concept is "pre-selling." What's to stop you from drawing sustenance from the customer pool before spending up your savings account on a risky business venture? Anything that can be done to reduce risk should be done, in my opinion. That's why I condone building a customer list before actually opening your doors.

The most overlooked sales method for a new cleaning business I have dubbed "Stalking." As an upstart you should make a foray into customer territory with the intent of carving out a niche, or if you prefer less gruesome terminology, to draw sustenance from the customer pool. Why wait until you've started your cleaning business to begin finding customers? You may go to the customer pool without owning it. Sneak up on it, study it, understand the customer pool before spending your precious savings.

Richard C. Meehan, Jr.

SALES FOR THE CLEANING AGENCY

To discuss selling in our World of Clean, we first need an understanding of the act of purchasing. All of us purchase things in order to survive, especially food. That's why we're labeled "consumers." Even the most stalwart purchasing agent cannot make better decisions than a mom on a tight budget shopping for clothes for her kids. Both are tough, shrewd, and sometimes, even logical in their buying habits. Their decisions are based on series of complex emotional stimuli. Sounds forbidding, doesn't it? Let's put it another way: my wife is cagey when it comes to spending money. She shops for the best price, haggles if possible to get the price down, but never buys junk no matter what the price. There is nothing simplistic about the act of purchasing, yet most cleaning services take a naive approach to selling.

If we rely solely on low prices to sell our services,

not only do we lose profits, we lose sales. Buyers seek value for their money. The trick is to convey the value attached to our service in ways buyers will understand. What it boils down to is an *emotional* appeal!

The act of shopping is fraught with emotions, especially if haggling is involved. This means a buyer's five senses must come into play during a sales presentation. Think about the last time you purchased a really great steak at the grocery store. Didn't you search for the best color on the meat, test the air around the butcher's counter with your nose to make sure there were no unsavory smells of putrefaction, poked at the plastic wrap to test for tenderness, and listen to the crinkle of the foam tray in your fingers? The only thing you couldn't do was taste the meat, yet I expect your mouth watered at the thought of doing so! You told yourself, based on the emotional responses from all the other physical sensations that you needed to buy that meat. Only then did logic take a stand.

At last, it gets down to reasoning. Can you afford it? Should you afford it? After all, a good porterhouse steak is rather expensive. Is it worth the price for that moment of palatability? You savor the taste in your mind again to make sure you really want it. Sometimes you do, sometimes you don't. I'll bet it's really hard to put that package back in the meat counter, though. Logic must take over in order to refuse a purchase that in every other way has been decided upon. You must tell yourself firmly, "I can't afford it...I don't really need this...I need something else instead..." A good salesperson can identify this final moment of indecision.

Let's continue with the porterhouse steak example: A good butcher would be watching for signs that a customer might be hesitant. "Putting together a special meal tonight? Need help deciding on the right choice of meat? Ah, planning a special treat for the grill, are you?" Questions like these, empathetic in nature, are designed to keep the customer on track in the final stage of purchasing—making the decision to buy. In this case, the butcher knows the customer wants a very good steak because he noticed signs of interest (visual scrutiny, fiddling with the package, a furrowed brow). The questions are couched to remind the customer of why she wants the steak. This kind of query must come at that  moment of hesitancy, when logic has nearly toppled the idea of making the purchase.

A person's body language can be most telling, like reading a book. We should watch our clients with an eye toward recognizing signs of stress. Every buyer goes through moments of hesitancy when it comes to spending money. Buying can be stressful, especially when the purchase represents a sizable amount of the cleaning budget—similar to buying a car, house, or even a porterhouse steak! The cost of our services versus the perceived affordability can be painful for our buyer. We should offer relief in the form of justification: if the customer needs what we offer, we must help them justify the purchase.

Selling is a combination of art, science, and religion. Good salespeople are moral in their dealings with others, so they don't take advantage of a client's indecision to push services that aren't really needed. We, owners or salespeople for our cleaning agency, should know our services and capabilities thoroughly, like medical doctors who understand details of anatomy necessary to triage, diagnose, a prescribe remedies for physical maladies. Finally, a service demonstration should have the qualities of a masterpiece: understandable theme, emotional evocation, and satisfaction through purchase. Yes, even cleaning firms should demonstrate their abilities as a way of satisfying a prospective client's desire for justification of monies allocated. We should show what we are capable of, not tell. Otherwise, what we describe about our services goes "in one ear and out the other," like Mom used to say.

Never let price be the overriding factor in selling services. Allow your firm's service benefits to be shown to a potential buyer in a manner that brings out the emotions necessary to make the decision to purchase. Be attentive for a prospective buyer's stressful moment of indecision and help channel that stress into a buying decision using empathetic questions. Know when to shut up. Too much input at that final indecisive moment can cause the loss of the sale. The salesperson who talks too much is usually labeled "pushy." Be helpful instead.

Selling is far more than a simple job; it is a profession that all businesses should embrace. Most cleaning service owners or their salespeople do not approach buyers as professionals though. Like all professionals, we must study to become experts on our services, bone up on sales techniques, observe carefully, listen hard, and demonstrate our capabilities. When a potential client has greater skills in these areas, it is far easier for the "NO" word to slip out. "The price is too high," is rarely the true reason for an offer being refused. Negative responses should always be viewed as a desire for more information, rather than a brick wall. If a customer truly wants the service, can afford it, and turns it down, shame on us for not knowing how to close the sale!

NO JOB TOO BIG OR TOO SMALL

I've got a pet peeve. Yes, and when someone strokes it without permission, I have to say something about it. My pet's name is "No Job Too Big or Too Small," or Nojob for short. Someone petted Nojob just the other day by mentioning how tough it is to get new business in this economy. After a few qualifying questions, I discovered that this particular small business person was going after mega-corps for cleaning jobs – exclusively. While this is a noble goal, most mega-corps have layers upon layers of red tape to cut through for one to finally get an opportunity even to be considered for making a quotation to possibly handle some of the cleaning business somewhere in the system, maybe. Put on your gloves boys and girls, because Nojob's getting ready to bite!

Unless your cleaning company is a national chain with mega-resources to match the needs of mega-corps, you need to take a step back and think. Layer Number One: if you don't have the ability to handle a particular type of client, don't take them on! This does not mean that at some point your company can't take the job, only that you take the job when you know beyond doubt that you can do a good one. Otherwise, you'll end up losing the new business. Not only that, but you'll damage your company's reputation. Building a good reputation in this industry, where word-of-mouth advertising can make or break a cleaning company, should be your biggest concern. Always do a fabulous job within your scope of abilities. Guard your reputation like an armored knight!

Layer Number Two involves product knowledge. You've heard me harp on this before. To quote from Sarris, the bad alien in the sci-fi spoof, <u>Galaxy Quest</u>, "You think that I am a fool, that the Commander does not know ever bolt, every weld, of his ship?" A cleaning contractor's product, or "ship," contains many facets, from accounting and inventory, to material safety, to proper cleaning methods, to human resources, to taxation, to sales techniques – it's all in the boat and much more. The trick is to continue to increase your knowledge of all areas in your vessel. With growth in your knowledge comes the *possibility* of growth in your business. Skills must be acquired, especially those pertaining to sales and presentation. Either you do it yourself, or you hire a professional salesperson to do it for you. However, if you hire a representative, make absolutely sure they understand not to oversell your company's abilities. See Layer

Number One.

Another consideration, Layer Number Three, is the avoidance of delusions of grandeur. We all start getting the "swelled head" after we've been stroked for doing a good job. Confidence builds, so we jump out to top the last good job with something even better. But, as Nojob can tell you from experience, this is a fleeting sensation that evaporates at the first sign of inability to complete a task. Not only do we lose our confidence, we start the mouths a'wagging about the poor performance we provided. For a salesperson, I would term this "salesperson slump." It is the downside of the bell curve, or the slippery slope of decreasing business. Stretching our muscles is fine; over-stretching causes pain and injuries. Grow a business of course; only make sure to build in a controlled fashion.

The idea that "no job is too big" is ludicrous, as I've just pointed out. What about small jobs though? Actually, Layer Number Four, or "no job is too small," has detrimental effects on our business too. This concerns the concept of Costing, or pricing our products and services. Let's take an example. The factors involved are thus:

1. My company has three employees including me, myself, and I.
2. I have one pickup truck loaded with sundry cleaning tools and products.
3. Five small offices, each with less than twenty employees, are the perfect size for me to handle.

4. I just obtained a new customer through word-of-mouth – a small church. I hated to turn them down because I could use the extra money.

Now, I'm heading out to go clean the church. It's about an hour's drive from my furthest small office, well outside of my normal route between jobs. The question: Is it worth it? Well, maybe, maybe not. It depends on the costs involved. Churches have lots of nooks and crannies, especially under pews and chairs. They take a lot of extra time and labor that normal office cleaning does not. Plus, there's the cost of travel and maintenance on the old truck to think about. Uh oh, and small churches normally don't have a lot of money to spend on cleaning maintenance, so the pay is low compared to the other business I already have. Hummmm, I don't want to upset anyone though, so I continue on my way to handle the job. With some newly acquired knowledge about costing my jobs, I still wonder if this is the right way to grow my business. Figures like these start rumbling through my head:

My hourly rate is based upon X dollars invested in cleaning chemicals, truck, gas, storage space rental, office equipment, cleaning equipment, bonded insurance, taxes, in short, the factors that detract money from my profits, termed "overhead." After I've tallied all that, I have to make at least $36.85 per hour to cover the overhead, fund my wage, and make a small profit to reinvest. I can handle cleaning each of these small offices in just under an hour per unit. The office units fall within the size range of about 500 square feet each. So, five hours times $36.85 divided by 2500 total square feet, means billing of about 7 cents per square foot. The jobs are simple and fairly easy on my back too.

I find that cleaning the church takes a full eight hours every week after 5:00 PM on Friday. Things have to be nice and tidy when the church opens for Sunday morning service, so this is the best time for my cleaning to occur. By multiplying my necessary hourly rate of $36.85 by 8, this totals $294.80 billed to the church. They are a little slow to pay, relying on donations as they do, but usually the check comes within thirty days. The church is actually 6200 square feet too, much bigger than the other jobs combined. Eight hours times $36.85 divided by 6200 square feet, means a billed rate of about 4.75 cents per square foot – that's 2.25 cents per square foot less money than the offices, and my back aches something fierce the rest of the weekend. Not only am I working longer and harder, but I'm actually taking half the pay, well below my threshold for making my wage after overhead. After careful consideration, I find that handling the church business is costing me money!

Sometimes it is necessary to walk away from prospective business to preserve the bottom line. These instances will become less frequent if you do the math up front before taking on more work. While the above example is fairly simplistic, peeling back the layers to get to the nitty-gritty is important. This is called qualifying the prospect, a staple philosophy in Selling.

Still think no job is too big or too small? No matter what mathematical formula you use to arrive at your bottom line, facts are facts. Some jobs are definitely too small and some jobs are ludicrously large. It is all based on your individual contracting company's costs of doing business. Everyone's company may be different, but the math works for all – even the one-horse operation. Do your best with what you have, but increase profits by increasing your knowledge. Insure that your reputation is paramount and secure all along the way by learning to screen jobs with grace; otherwise, they will cut into your profits. Grow into larger jobs as you obtain the necessary tools of education and equipment. Don't end up like Nojob – dejected, neglected, angry...and out of business. Muzzle the beast by doing the diligence of qualifying your prospective customers before taking on the extra work!

SPRING CLEANING EXPOSED

Okay, so you've got some steady clientele and your cleaning business is on a roll. That's great, wonderful, and superb! But, are you milking those clients for all they are worth? Git it whilst the git'ins good – as long as *it* is mutually beneficial. That's my motto. Well? They don't call it "spring cleaning" for nothing! Now is the time to ask for extra work from those steady accounts, not to lay back and soak up the sunshine while your competitor garners your business.

For those of you who mainly contract for outside cleaning, get some inside jobs. Likewise, you domestic folks need to pull some extra profits from outside scrub-ups. This is called "adding on." Like, duh. The fact is, add-on services are the most overlooked profit centers for any type of business. You've already done the tough part by garnering customers from a fickle marketplace, so why haven't you continued to sell them on new stuff that you can do? Every season offers a different set of opportunities for adding on new cleaning jobs, but springtime beats them all!

Learning to ask for more business from existing customers is perhaps the most important aspect of keeping them. A contracting firm's public representative, whether it's the owner or a hired salesperson, is responsible for bringing in the bounty. So why is it that asking for more business is so difficult? It's not really, just overlooked. In the hustle and bustle of daily servicing, we forget that customers have to be engaged or else they get bored with us. To prevent a good customer from looking elsewhere for excitement, it is our representative's job

Kristina Meehan, author's daughter, doesn't mind hard work.

to keep them busy – by stimulating them with new opportunities for cleanliness – especially in the spring.

Spring weather is good in several ways: the outside temperature is comfortable, the inside climate is looking outward at the return of greenery; people get the urge to make things happen; excitement fills the air. Remember how it was sitting in that classroom on a brilliant spring day, watching the rustling of the new leaves filled with chirping birds, feeling the sunshine through the window, while trying to concentrate on the latest algebra problem in a stuffy classroom with a stuffy teacher? (My wife is a teacher, so she won't let me get away with this one.) Antsy! And, this is how your customers feel right now!

Take advantage of Spring Fever by offering up some extras to keep your customers focused on what you do for them; otherwise, your competitor might just sneak a foot in the door by offering to do these things in your stead. Don't forget that as add-on services, this means add-on charges too. Price and bill these things separately.

Here's a short list of ideas:

- ✓ Window washing, both inside and out
- ✓ Concrete and sidewalk cleaning
- ✓ Extract winter mud from the carpets and entry mats
- ✓ Shine up the floors after a long winter's abuse
- ✓ Polish old brass door knobs
- ✓ Scrub ceramic tile and stone to remove wet weather grime
- ✓ Pressure clean the outside of the building
- ✓ Detail interior walls, especially around ductwork and doors
- ✓ Wash the outbuildings
- ✓ Minor to major landscaping projects
  - o Clients hate to deal with many different contractors
  - o If you don't handle yard maintenance, consider subcontracting
- ✓ Sweep the garage

- ✓ Box possessions for clients that may be moving
- ✓ Minor to major painting projects
  - ○ See above reasoning and partnering
- ✓ Minor building repair projects
  - ○ See above reasoning and partnering

A really wise thing to do would be to create a spring add-on flyer listing your extra services. Don't put prices on these handouts, though. Always create a special contract for special services, priced by the job.

Extra work during the spring is available right now, so once your list is complete, put it in the hands of your regulars pronto. When it comes to labor for the new work, pay overtime or hire more people. After all, spring only comes once a year. Besides, if your company can handle all of the spring cleaning needs of your clients, there is less of a chance that one of your competitors will be able to plunk a foot in your door. Of course, it is always best to stick with what you know. That's why I'm a proponent of continual education. If I don't know how to do it, I learn. Think of self-education as self-preservation.

Speaking of preservation, if your competitor isn't offering spring cleaning add-ons, you've been handed the Golden Opportunity to inch your foot in their door. As U.S. Attorney General Erik Holder once said, "You never want a serious crisis go to waste." That's exactly what it is when a competitor misses out on your Spring Cleaning *Extra*vaganza – a crisis for them – so git it whilst the git'ins good!

TAKE THAT TO THE BANK!

I suppose you've figured out by now that I harp on acquiring more knowledge to increase profits in our contract cleaning companies. Although it has a wonderful sound – p...r...o...f...i...t...s – many of you simply do not understand what I'm driving at. Let's face it, the cleaning industry as a whole has a reputation for employing educationally challenged personnel. Many owners barely made it through high school, much less college. Few janitors and maids reached beyond high school. None of this really matters in the world of cleaning, especially if you understand that this industry is as much a trade as bricklaying or carpentry. A good cleaning person learns tricks of the trade from someone with more experience. It may not take a lot of studying to sling a mop or scrub with a brush, but a true professional can make a facility look so good that it sings without a diploma. Unfortunately, to run a cleaning business it takes far more than manual labor done properly.

Although no one can really get enough schooling, knowledge is not simply about books. Knowledge is about information and wisdom. You can take that to the bank!

Of course, what any good business owner wants is take more money to the bank. If some of that money gets to stay there instead of being spent on the costs of doing business, that's really great. This excess is called profit. Since the contract cleaning trade is a hands-on field, anything that makes it more rewarding is a good thing. Obviously, moneymaking is what the trade is all about. So how do you turn a higher profit? Are you afraid I'm getting ready to say "crack the books?" Well, actually I am – you can take that to the bank too.

To soften the blow, let me tell a personal story. My son, at age 21, joined the U.S. Army. His reasoning, "I don't like college and I don't want to waste any more of your money, Daddy." Well, I appreciate saving some money, for sure. However, I know enough about the U.S. Army from friends and family that have served to know that training never stops. Some of that training is done in the classroom. My son picked a field that requires tremendous volumes of book-learning, testing, field training, and more testing. All this is to keep him as safe as possible, and I am truly thankful for that. One of his phone calls was, "I'm learning a lot, especially since I have spent eight hours a day for the last five weeks in the classroom." If I can't lead a horse to water and make him drink, the U.S. Army surely can...and you can take that to the bank!

Now, I can't force-feed knowledge and wisdom into

you, but I surely can lead you to the trough. Resources for the cleaning industry are boundless these days. When I first started in the trade, virtually nothing was available except a couple of magazines and maybe a book or two at the public library. Since the advent of the World Wide Web, every form of media has hopped onboard to educate the cleaning industry. People like me are flooding the system daily with tips and tricks, how-to manuals, videos, books, e-zines, websites – you name it. The trade is inundated with a smorgasbord of information. Big words for an unlearned occupation; however, like my son, I implore you to educate yourself in whatever fashion works best for you. Along with your education level your profits will rise, and you can take that to the bank.

Here is a list of my top ten favorite resources to help increase my product knowledge:

1) Trade magazines, both printed and on the web: www.ecleanmag.com; www.cleanlink.com, run by Trade Press, publisher of *Sanitary Maintenance*; www.maintenancesalesnews.com, by Rankin Publishing, publisher of *Maintenance Sales News*.

2) Your local public library in the "building maintenance" section.

3) YouTube (www.youtube.com) where you can search for videos on virtually every cleaning machine and procedure.

4) Manufacturers' websites list resource materials on their products – how to, specification sheets, material safety data, sales flyers, seminars, training sessions.

5) <u>Secrets</u> <u>of</u> <u>Closing</u> <u>the</u> <u>Sale</u>, by Zig Ziglar, world famous sales trainer and motivational speaker, now deceased. His sales methods are timeless, however.

6) Cleaning associations offer resources and training events. The largest of these is the International Sanitary Supply Association, or ISSA (<u>www.issa.com</u>).

7) Your local janitorial supply house is the place to get one-on-one instruction, mostly for free.

8) Janitorial and cleaning staff working in the trenches every day. Some of them are masters willing to train apprentices. Learn from them.

9) Government agencies like OSHA, EPA, DOT, and USDA contain the rules and regulations governing occupational, environmental, transportation, and food safety. Cleaning procedures and materials handling are greatly affected by these laws. Those who ignore them get put out of business.

10) To study up on changes in the laws governing business operations, use the Federal Register, <u>www.federalregister.gov.</u>

No one ever said it would be easy to run a cleaning business. In addition to the resources above, it is wise to have local investment advisors, bankers, lawyers, accountants, insurance agents, and even other cleaning company professionals in your repertoire of consultants. I have been told by many cleaning pros who started off as apprentices and worked their way into becoming masters that they never had a clue about the level of expertise it takes to run a cleaning business until they tried it for themselves. The story is one about the School of Hard Knocks, so you can take that to the bank.

Now that we've about reached the fall of the year, many of us are evaluating where our profits stand so far. Are we better off than last year to date? How are we going to improve our profits in the years to come? One of my favorite old television shows was a police drama called *Baretta*, which aired from 1975 to 1978. The main character, a New Jersey plainclothes detective named Tony Baretta, held the answer to staying in business (surviving in a tough world). He was pragmatic; hence, his favorite phrase, "You can take that to the bank!" He meant what he said and backed it up using whatever force necessary to bring a successful outcome to the situation. It was the force of willpower, just the same as the power needed to buckle down to study. Studying is the path to Knowledge; Wisdom comes from experience on the streets. So, starting right now, this fall, hit the Information Highway to discover what it will take to increase your profits and stay in business. Otherwise, like so many undereducated cleaning contractors, this fall may be your last – and you can take that to the bank!

A BRISTLY SUBJECT

Push brooms are perhaps the most popular cleaning tools on the planet next to mops; therefore, it is important as a cleaning contractor to have an arsenal of them to draw from on a moment's notice. Time is

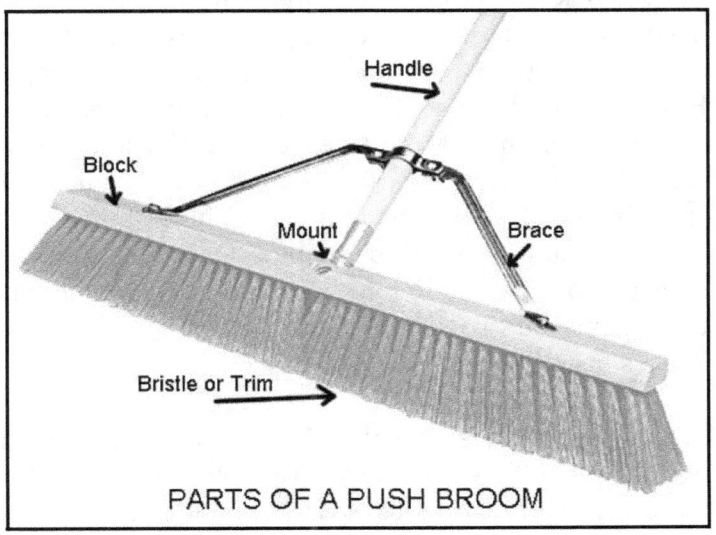

PARTS OF A PUSH BROOM

money in our industry, so wasting it in search of a push broom can be costly. It would be prudent to stock a small quantity of each size and bristle type to avoid downtime too. As with other cleaning tools, a push broom must be matched to the person handling the job. Make the decision now to keep a variety stashed so you are prepared for unexpected circumstances.

SIZE

Push brooms come in limited shapes and sizes. They are long and thin with handles, bristles, and sometimes braces. Lengths vary from around 12" to 36" long by 2" to 3-1/2" wide. A push broom block is the part that holds the bristles in place. Blocks come in wood, fiberglass, plastic, or metal. Handles are available in several diameters ranging from 3/4" to 1-1/4", and lengthwise between 54" and 64" long. The handle materials can be wood, fiberglass, plastic, or metal (sometimes wrapped in a plastic coating). Handles also mount to blocks using differing methods, the most common being threaded (screws into block receptacle). Braces are used to reduce the chances of snapping handles off, reaming out the block threads, or breaking various types of mounts. Once this kind of breakage occurs, the broom is usually a goner and has to be replaced. To increase the life of your brooms, always install braces. *

* If you have a further interest in how this valuable cleaning tool is made, please view the YouTube video posted by the Discovery Channel, How It's Made: Push Brooms.

FIT

When choosing a broom to fit the user, make sure to pick the appropriate size. A little elderly lady cannot push a 36" long broom weighing six pounds for very long. It would wear her out too quickly, or even get her hurt. However, the same broom in an 18" length weighing in at two pounds would probably be the better choice. Once the proper size is chosen, then pick the right bristle for the job. Even if the job is large, a broom that is inappropriate for the user will slow down the cleaning process. Fatigue is a factor when choosing size. If a smaller broom fits the person better, he  or she will be able to work longer without fatigue. It is of course beneficial to look at broom size in the opposite direction too. A long, heavy push broom would certainly cover a lot more area in a shorter time if the user can handle it without undue stress. Larger can be faster – if the person can handle the weight.

FIBER MATERIALS

Fibers for push brooms run from natural to synthetics, each filament type designed for a particular purpose. As with all cleaning jobs, the surface to be cleaned should determine the correct choice of cleaning materials and equipment – not the other way around. Too many times I have witnessed people overworking themselves simply because they weren't using the proper bristle for the task. Usually this is in the name of saving money. Tell me: Which is more expensive, cost of labor or cost of tools? When a job calls for a soft bristle, a stiff bristle simply will not do; likewise, the opposite. Have you ever tried to push gravel or remove dust using a broom that simply would not move the debris? What a waste of time! With high labor costs these days, ANY tool that cuts significant time from a cleaning task is of great value. Again, keep a good stock of broom types. It's cheaper that way simply because they help the job get done in a timelier fashion.

Why are there so many bristle fibers to choose from? Stiffness to match debris types, liquid

Polypropylene bristle with straight filament

retention for scrubbing purposes, durability, and cost are just a few of the characteristics that make certain fibers better for certain jobs. From dusting floors to scoring fresh concrete, push broom fibers have one thing in common: resilience. I personally own a horsehair push broom that is as old as I am, and I use it weekly to sweep my smooth concrete garage floor. If I had instead used it on rough ceramic tile, the bristles would have worn out in a few months. Match bristle types to the job.

Acrylic is a resilient, pliable, synthetic fiber which can resist a bit of heat, acid, and most solvents without melting. The fiber bends readily, yet springs back to original form quickly (memory). It is available in flagged soft bristles that remove fine dust. Flagged tips means the fiber has been feathered on the ends. This lends acrylics the ability to push fine particles with little filtering through the broom. Flagged acrylic push brooms can even be used to replace dust mops. However, acrylics do not work well with sweeping compounds containing oil, nor do they perform satisfactorily on oily surfaces like automotive shops. Push brooms with acrylic bristles work great for fine dust and lightweight debris removal from smooth surfaces.

Acrylic bristle with flagged tips

Bristles are usually trimmed to 3" in length, which offers excellent "snap-back" flexibility. Consider this: one of the features of any broom is the ability of its fiber to return to original position when the broom is lifted from the floor. That simple motion propels debris ahead of the broom and shakes particulates from the broom fiber, a self-cleaning action. Acrylic push brooms are considered fine sweeping tools.

A step up in stiffness is the very resilient polypropylene synthetic fiber. This bristle is available in a wide range of colors, thicknesses, and crimped or straight fiber varieties. With a high resistance to acids and solvents, polypropylene bristles are good for automotive situations where liquids varying from water to petroleum oils get bound up in dust and debris. For the ultimate "wet area" broom, choose polypropylene bristles mounted in plastic blocks. Thinner polypropylene bristles are touted as medium sweep brooms, and work well for debris ranging from

slightly finer than sand to small gravel. Crimped bristles hold moisture and are excellent for pushing wet, coarse

Polypropylene bristle with crimped filament

material. Coupled with a scattering of oil-based sweeping compound (sawdust and oil), this fiber makes a great choice for medium sweeping on wet or dry, smooth to moderately rough surfaces.

Polypropylene is also available in the ultimate street broom stiffness too. With thicker bristles made for moving rough, gravely material, street brooms must withstand coarse, wet surfaces without becoming soft. The crimped bristle style also allows for heavy duty scrubbing by holding detergents better while working. This bristle is the ultimate for rough duty work.

Tampico, a natural fiber derived from the Agave Lechugilla plant of arid northern Mexico, is a medium-soft bristle material with a smooth, yet slightly abrasive texture. This combo makes for an excellent medium sweep general purpose broom that holds up to uncoated concrete and other semi-rough surfaces over long periods. The fiber becomes soft in

Tampico natural fiber

water and other liquids, so this type of broom should be used in dry or limited-wet areas only. Tampico holds moisture and must be allowed to dry before the bristles will stiffen again. Bristle life is very long life though with a good resistance to acids and most solvents. For the perfect "mostly dry" warehouse broom, couple this bristle with oil-based sweeping compounds.

BLOCKS

Fibers can be set into structural foam plastic, wood, or aluminum blocks, all of which come in a variety of styles and sizes, as we have seen. Synthetic block materials are resistant to moisture and do not warp or splinter like wood. Hardwood blocks are the traditional material with only one real drawback: when

43

run over by a forklift or equivalent heavy machine they can bust. Plastic block brooms usually survive the pressure, but metal blocks can bend. To recap: there are several different types of push brooms (also called floor brushes) available. Indoor sweeps, garage sweeps, and street sweeps are the main categories, or fine, medium, and rough if you prefer. In addition, each of these categories contain a variety of bristle styles and sizes. For larger brooms is always

Dual bristle types on plastic block

best to use braces for added handle support. This prevents undue wear on the block from twisting and turning. Small block lengths below 18" do not usually require braces, but anything longer should sport at least one brace. After all, once the handle mount is worn out, so goes the broom.

HANDLES AND BRACES

Although this article is not really about handles and braces, push brooms without them are nothing more than hand-held scrub brushes; therefore, I offer a few recommendations to save much money in the long haul:

- ➢ Buy only quality push brooms based on the information in this article.
- ➢ Couple them with quality handles with good threaded tips.
- ➢ Add a small brace for short brooms.
- ➢ Add a long triangle brace for long brooms.
- ➢ For the ultimate brooms, add both small and triangle braces with steel-tipped handles.

Quality brooms can be expensive up front. If you are in a cleaning business and expect to be in that business for the long run, use the proper equipment for the job and not the cheapest thing you can get your hands on. Invest in good brooms! The savings found by

Large and small braces save brooms!

getting the job done faster and better with less pain and fatigue far outweigh the upfront costs. As one of the premier tools of the cleaning trade, push brooms rank up there as highly important, but least respected. Change that attitude by spending a bit of time finding good brooms. Keep a variety of bristles styles and block

Get good handles to prevent breakage of either the handle or the broom.

lengths in stock to grab quickly. Match brooms to people first and then to the job. A broom in hand is worth two in the bush, so avoid downtime by having proper brooms nearby. A little attention to this important cleaning tool will set you on the road to greater profits.

Richard C. Meehan, Jr.

ANATOMY OF A RESTROOM

Whether you call them restrooms, bathrooms, loos, dunnies, or other endearments, one thing's for sure, these personal spaces are the most germ-ridden of all places. Oh look, I'm a poet and didn't know it. Here's an axiom: cleaning professionals that do a great job of sanitizing restrooms not only insure future repeat business, but perform sheer poetry when it comes to facility cleanliness. Nothing dampens a first impression faster in a home or business than an unpleasant aroma drifting from the W.C. Remember, cleanliness is next to Godliness, and disagreeable odors must be eliminated to insure a sense of wholesomeness. Goodness gracious, I'm waxing philosophical too.

If you are a cleaning professional assigned the task of making a restroom sparkle, then you are the key to your company's future business from that client. Of all the maintenance chores, this is the most dreaded and hated. Why? Well, not only is it in many cases a nasty job, but it takes a special person to ignore the stigma associated with cleaning commodes and other restroom fixtures. It takes an attitude adjustment, that's what! To quote actor Will Smith from *Men in Black*, "First off, you chose me...so you recognize the skills." Will's character was pointing out that he deserved respect for his talents. Anyone who performs a superior job in the wonderful world of restroom maintenance should be venerated, praised, admired, and rewarded.

A cleaning firm that can consistently perform superior work in this key area insures a customer's gratitude. Of course, there are always those folks that can never be satisfied. In the grand scheme of continued business, that client type should probably be let go in favor of doing a better job for others who recognize the skills. That's where the profit will be. Therefore, it is imperative to instruct cleaning staff on the proper methods of cleaning restrooms. Don't allow shoddy cleaning procedures to take a bite out of your profitability.

Before we talk about these procedures, let's identify surfaces that harbor germs in all restrooms and bathrooms. Here is a list including various material types to be expected, whether in a home or commercial facility:

- **Doors:** doorknobs, door panels
- **Walls:** splash areas around sinks, commodes, and urinals
- **Floors:** vinyl, ceramic tile, stone, concrete, composite, and wood

- **Ceilings:** ductwork and vents
- **Sinks:** porcelain, chrome, brass, copper, fiberglass, plastic
- **Dispensers:** towels, toilet tissue, hand soap, hygiene units, seat covers
- **Mirrors:** includes all glass
- **Trash Cans:** inside, outside, lids, and sanitary napkin disposal units
- **Fixtures:** commodes, urinals, and bidets
- **Showers:** ceramic tile, vinyl, porcelain, stone, plastic, fiberglass
- **Tubs:** ceramic tile, porcelain, plastic, fiberglass
- **Matting:** carpet, vinyl, polyester
- **Baby Changing Stations:** plastic
- **Deodorant systems and dispensers:** solid, liquid, gel, and aerosol
- **Grout:** found in various places in a restroom, wherever a water seal is needed

While not every facility has all of the above components, it is a sure bet that a cleaning company must go prepared for all of these situations. Thankfully, the materials required will work in nearly all cases. If a cleaning company has the proper equipment and chemicals for handling the restroom, at least that means they have nearly everything they need for the rest of the facility too. The bathroom requires the most intense use of cleaning products and labor; thus, efficient procedures reduce overall costs.

When dealing with a bathroom, no matter the size or location, the following procedure will obtain a high level of cleanliness – with a conscientious person behind the elbow grease. Train your restroom people well.

CLEANERS REQUIRED:

1. <u>All Purpose Disinfectant</u>: A professional quality neutral cleaner, deodorizer, and disinfectant all-in-one. These come in a variety of deodorants, but contain basically the same active disinfectant. The active ingredient is quaternary ammonium chloride, commonly called quat.

2. <u>Non-Acid, Mild Acid, Acid Porcelain Cleaner</u>: Although porcelain should always be cleaned with a non-acid product, which has not always been the case in the past. Porcelain can stain and be the devil to clean. Once an acid is used, it becomes likely that from that point, acid will always have to be used on that fixture to get it clean. Rule of thumb: use the weakest product that will get the job done to avoid further damage to the porcelain.

3. <u>Pumice Sticks</u>: These handy little tools will not scratch porcelain. They are perfect for removing the toughest stains, even rust, from old or new porcelain fixtures.

4. <u>Foaming Germicidal Cleaner Aerosol</u>: Although aerosols are more expensive for the same basic chemicals as liquids, sometimes the speed factor outweighs the extra expense. Labor hours are costlier than cleaners.

5. <u>Hospital Disinfectant Spray</u>: Using the same reasons as above, these products are fast drying, quick

to permeate, and eliminate odors in hard-to-reach places.

6. <u>Glass and Plexi-glass Cleaner</u>: There is a choice between liquid and aerosol here. My personal preference is liquid glass cleaner in restrooms because liquids are less expensive. Avoid ammonia based cleaners here mainly because ammonia can cause damage to Plexi-glass and plastic surfaces along the nature of permanent fogging.

7. <u>Enzyme-based Deodorant-Digestant</u>: These products usually contain a pleasant deodorant, but that's not why we need them – it's the enzymes. Organic matter, from feces, to urine, to bacteria, cause odors in restrooms. These enzymes break down the odor-causing bacteria just as they do in a septic system.

8. <u>Graffiti Remover</u>: This is an indispensable aerosol product for the removal of inks, dyes, lip stick, markers, glues, and other damaging materials from restroom stalls and fixtures.

9. <u>Household Bleach</u>: CAUTION. AVOID USING BLEACH AND BLEACH-BASED CLEANERS EXCEPT WHEN ABSOLUTELY NECESSARY. Bleach damages many surfaces, tracks easily where it doesn't belong, is unhealthy to breathe, and isn't very compatible around other chemicals, especially ammonia. However, sometimes it is needed to remove stains in latex grout where the grout has been damaged by mildew.

10. <u>Household Ammonia</u>: DON'T USE, PERIOD.

11. <u>Solid, Liquid or Aerosol Deodorizer</u>: These are optional; however, nothing pleases a customer more than a pleasant experience when visiting the restroom. I highly recommend a deodorant system (more on this later).

<u>EQUIPMENT REQUIRED</u>:

1. <u>Microfiber Flat Mop System</u>: While not necessarily efficient in large areas, flat mops are great for most restrooms. The exceptions might run to football stadiums or airports where fifty-stall restrooms are not uncommon. Flat mops offer a simple solution to a thorny problem. Mops contaminate chemicals and harbor germs themselves. Flat mops are easily changed, never dipped in cleaning solution after initially saturated, outlast regular mops, and are easily laundered. Put simply, they perform well for disinfection processes where cross-contamination of materials is a problem.

2. <u>Microfiber Cloths or Disposable Wipers</u>: I am a proponent of microfiber. The material outlasts standard terry towel rags and other forms of cellulose wipers. Microfiber cloths are launder-able innumerable times. This means in the long run they are less expensive to use.

3. <u>Toilet Bowl and Urinal Brushes</u>: Wrapped-wire bowl and urinal brushes with extensions, commercial grade, offer the strength of bristle needed to actually clean most commodes, urinals, and bidets, without having to use harsh acid-based cleaners.

4. <u>Trigger Sprayer or Small Pump Sprayers</u>: Disinfectant and other liquid cleaners should be pre-diluted in these handle little devices. Sprayers offer exceptional control over the amount of chemicals and liquids applied to a restroom. These are major cost-saving tools.

5. <u>Stick Broom and Lobby Dust Pan</u>: This equipment is the fastest way to remove heavier debris like wadded paper and dust bunnies from a restroom floor. They may not always be necessary

6. <u>Janitor Cart or Dolly</u> (OPTIONAL): Depending on the size of the facility, a cart may be necessary in order to carry all of the accoutrements needed to clean a restroom. Never allow the cleaning staff to do the Janitor's Shuffle, from car to job and back again. This takes too much time away from the cleaning effort. Time is money. Determine the best way to get all of the required cleaners, tools, tissues, towels, etc. to the location as efficiently as possible.

7. <u>Supply Refillables (Add-On Sales)</u>: Don't lose the opportunity to add on to the cleaning contract by offering, at an extra charge of course, to refill all restroom dispensers. Hand soap, towels, toilet tissue, trash bags, deodorant refills, urinal floor mats – these and other common usage items offer extra profit points.

8. <u>Gloves and Goggles</u>: Every cleaning chemical used has some form of safety gear requirement. Refer to your Material Safety Data Sheets for further information. In general, always wear protective gloves! I like latex commercial grade disposable gloves that can easily be removed and thrown away between jobs.

This reduces contamination risks to people, places, and things.

9. <u>Stepladder</u>: A handy tool in case overhead work such as vent cleaning must be done.

10. <u>Acrylic Extension Duster</u>: This tool makes short work of spider webs, dust on vents, ceiling lights, and other restroom furnishings that may not like to be cleaned with water-based chemicals. Always clean the duster after use by swishing out in pre-diluted leftover disinfectant and hanging to dry.

11. <u>Large Cellulous Sponge</u>: Invaluable for swiping areas that cannot withstand lots of water.

12. <u>Hand-held Scrub Brush</u>: Useful around fixtures where soap scum and other buildup may be an issue.

13. <u>Scrubbing Machine (Optional)</u>: Depending on the size of your job, assistive machinery may speed up your process. A good example is when it becomes necessary to detail the grout lines on a ceramic tile floor.

14. <u>Deck Scrub Brush on a Handle:</u> This tool is usually needed in tile restrooms where grout lines can be a problem. If the job is too small for a scrubbing machine, then a deck brush can still take care of the situation.

<u>THE RESTROOM CLEANING PROCEDURE</u>
Throughout the entire procedure listed here it is assumed that the cleaning person will be using these basic products for most tasks: a sprayer of pre-diluted cleaner-deodorizer-disinfectant and a microfiber

system including cloths, mops, and bucket unless otherwise noted.

- PREREQUESITS
  - Follow instructions on cleaning chemicals and make sure they are prepared for use in sprayers or other containers.
  - Make sure all necessary cleaning equipment is handy (loaded caddies, carts, etc.).
  - Remove all trash cans and any other furnishings (if possible) from the area to be disinfected.
  - Empty all soiled materials from mounted trash cans, sanitary napkin disposal units, and floor model receptacles. (If the area is large, it is more efficient to empty refuse into a nearby janitor cart hopper or rolling trash receptacle.)
  - Dispose of all expended urinal and toilet floor mats, urinal screens, deodorant canisters, hanging commode blocks, etc.
  - Sweep any heavy debris from the floor with a stick broom and lobby dust pan.
  - Remove dispenser towels, toilet tissue, facial wipes, deodorants, seat covers, etc. to prevent them from becoming wet and unusable. They will be replaced once disinfection is near completion.

- STEP ONE – ABOVE THE WAIST OR THEREABOUT
  - If any ceiling work is needed, such as removing dust and mildew from vent fan covers, swishing away spider webs, cleaning light fixtures or

other high objects, do this now. *TIP: Spider webs are easily removed with an inexpensive extension acrylic duster.*

- If fingerprints or smudges need to be cleaned from walls or doors, now is the time. However, we will disinfect the door knobs as we leave.

- If graffiti is present, use the aerosol graffiti remover now.

- Depending on the wall surface type, lightly apply disinfectant to counters, sinks, urinals and commodes inside and out, and wall splash areas around those fixtures. Allow disinfectant to soak a minimum of five minutes in order to kill germs. If walls are made of sheetrock or another permeable material, wipe splash areas to remove excess moisture. Alternatively, use a sponge or wiper to gently scrub the walls in the splash zones. DO NOT SKIP THIS STEP because of inconvenience, as walls are easily damaged by acidic urine. Walls also become odor sources.

- After the required "dwell" or "soak" time listed on the disinfectant label has passed, wipe away the excess. This is the time to scrub problem areas such as around the hand soap dispensers, swish out the toilets and urinals.

- Finish cleaning all surfaces above the knee, paying particular attention to the facings of dispensers.

- STEP TWO – MOVING ON DOWN
- Using the sprayer, apply disinfecting solution to the floor. If the microfiber flat mop goes dry during mopping, simply spray down more solution. (Please note that we are not restoring tile and grout here, only

cleaning thoroughly. Restoration will be for another article.)

• After the required dwell time has been reached, use the pre-moistened microfiber pads according to manufacturer instructions to mop the floor. These systems are designed to be "touch-free" if used properly, which is safer for the user and reduces the chance of cross-contamination of chemicals, equipment, and even rooms.

• Remember to change out dirty flat mops as needed. Be sure to use clean pads, rags, and wipers too. A three-stall restroom with two urinals and two sinks, given an industrial situation where grease is present can require up to five flat mops. Carry the number of flat mops that will complete the task without having to waste time washing them out on the fly.

• Work toward the exit door.

• If odors are an issue, as soon as the floor cleaning is completed, grab the sprayer of Enzyme-based Deodorant-Digestant. Pump several squirts of Enzymes into the toilet and close the lid. Spray the inside of the urinals thoroughly. Lightly apply Enzymes to splash areas on the walls and floors. (If the walls are sheetrock or other surface harmed by excess water, use a sponge or wiper instead.)

• Refill all paper product, hand soap, deodorant, seat cover, and hygiene dispensers, and install fresh trash bags to mounted trash cans. Add all accessories like floor protective mats and urinal screens. Restore furnishings to original positions.

- Clean the inside and outside of all floor model trash cans. Replace the trash bags in the cans. Restore trash cans to original positions. If restroom odors are an issue, apply a few squirts of Enzyme-based Deodorant-Digenstant to the INSIDE of the trash bag liner.

- Remove all cleaning materials that may still be in area back to the carrier or cart.

- As the final task, clean the doorknobs. Close the door. Why? This indicates that the restroom has been sanitized. The next person in begins the process of re-contamination. Move on to the next area to be cleaned.

- **STEP THREE – CLEANUP OF EQUIPMENT USED**

- This is very simple. Cleaning equipment must be sanitized before the next job.

- Use the left over disinfectant to spray down the cart, buckets, tools, in short, every piece of cleaning equipment.

- Allow the proper dwell time. Rinse the cleaning equipment.

- Wash the microfiber flat mops and rags in disinfectant either by hand or with a machine. DO NOT USE BLEACH!

- Store equipment in a clean facility. What good is sanitized cleaning equipment if it is re-contaminated by a dirty janitor closet?

Is it necessary to perform all these tasks in every situation? Emphatically yes! Remember, germs know no limits except that of disinfection, and germs cause illness as well as unpleasant odors. Don't skimp in the restrooms as this is where your cleaning company can be broken.

We've talked a lot about procedures. It all boils down to one thing: proper restroom cleaning is an art backed by scientific fact. Fact #1: germs create issues concerning health. Fact #2: most restrooms are never fully disinfected which puts visitors at risk. Fact #3: cleaning staff in general dread the task of sanitizing these very human spaces because they get negative remarks – which can usually be resolved by giving them proper training. Fact #4: customers complain about unclean restrooms constantly and quite faithfully tell their friends about the terrible job the janitorial service has done. And Fact #5: when a restroom, or whatever you want to call it, is properly cleaned to poetic perfection, you don't have to philosophize on the wholesomeness it exudes. It just is – clean. Cleanliness makes the Higher Power happy. Keep those W.C.'s sparkling to keep your customers enthralled with your inspired labor.

MICROFIBER FLAT MOP SYSTEM SAVINGS

Microfiber flat mops are the most durable mopping products on the market. So what's the big deal? It's a touch-less system. That means you don't have to mess with the contaminated mop with your hands. It also means that your clean mops are never mixed with your dirty ones. When it comes to sanitization, a regular string mop or dust mop won't come anywhere close to matching the ease of use and versatility of a microfiber flat mop. There's only one

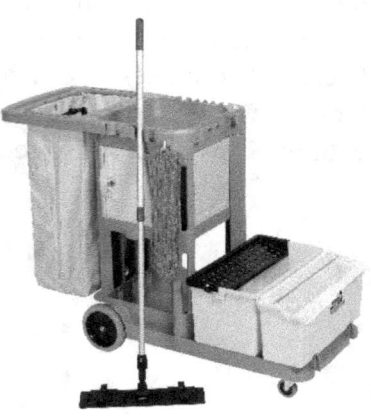

Continental Brand Janitor Cart with Microfiber Mop System

drawback: flat mop systems are only efficient in moderate to small areas. Clean rooms, hospital rooms, doctor's offices, and multi-stall restrooms are great examples of spots to use microfiber flat mop systems.

Microfiber, the material used to create quality flat mops, is made from polyester fibers which are split during production to produce voids in each strand. This makes the fiber soft, tough for scrubbing, and porous so it will hold dust, dirt, and liquids without releasing until the mop is washed under running water or in a laundry. Microfiber mops leave no lint either, nor do they fall apart, even after uncounted washes. The components of a flat mop system are:

- microfiber flat mop heads
- frame
- handle, either extension-style or straight
- dual bucket with strainer (cleaning solution, dirty mop disposal)

BENEFITS OF MICROFIBER FLAT MOP SYSTEMS:

1. Handles with the ease of a dust mop.
2. Works great in tight places.
3. Prevents cross-contamination.
4. Hands don't touch used mop heads: touch-less.
5. Extremely portable.
6. Economizes on expensive chemicals.
7. Fast cleaning without back strain.
8. No need to lug gallons of water.
9. Fits on a janitor cart for mobility.

10. More thorough than either dust mop or wet mop.
11. Indefinitely washable.
12. Can be used on walls, floors, and ceilings.
13. Low water use means floors dry faster.
14. Quick changeover to fresh mop head.
15. Most systems can double as a super floor finish application method.

Using Ben Franklin's favorite decision-making process, the pros outweigh cons; therefore, don't hesitate to get a set of these babies to immediately save money in cleaning chemicals and labor costs. They're fast and reliable.

Richard C. Meehan, Jr.

DO YOU HAVE ALL THE BUSINESS YOU CAN STAND?

The surest way to lose customers is to give them a reason to doubt your integrity. It doesn't take much, just a single instance of seeming untruth, and they're gone. This can happen in a variety of insipid ways. The question you should ask yourself whenever tempted to stretch the boundaries of truthfulness is, "Do you have all the business you can stand?" I'll bet the answer will always be negative. Unfortunately, there are thorns to prune if you wish to maintain a high level of trust with your customers.

Common sense is the best shear to cut away your prickly temptations. Little things will cost you the most. Here are some prime examples:

➢ Reading the contents on a buyer's desktop or computer when making the sales call is a big NO – restrain your roving eyes.

➢ Listening through the door to private conversations between a buyer and another supplier – tune your ears to filter out unrelated conversation; listen carefully to what the buyer has to say TO YOU.

➢ Browsing a buyer's workplace like a nosey mother-in-law – this is a distraction from your task, RUDE, and none of your business.

➢ Pestering other personnel at the buyer's facility about details pertaining to the buyer – see "NOSEY mother-in-law" above.

➢ Selling to a buyer who is not authorized to purchase your products – this is TAKING ADVANTAGE of a situation for your benefit and not the customer's.

➢ Overstocking a weak buyer for padding monthly sales totals is DISHONEST.

➢ Creating confusion over pricing and quantity in order to sell more is like ROBBING from Peter to pay Paul.

➢ Not anticipating problems that could arise through use of your product and failure to NOTIFY the buyer about them prior to the sale – Example: the customer mounted the new towel dispenser in the restroom too high for children and mobility impaired patrons.

➢ Committing to service after the sale that is not feasible – PUMPING UP what you are capable of doing.

➢ Overselling product features to mislead the buyer into thinking the product is better than it actually is – this is called "HYPING" or "selling the warranty" and is a sure way to disappoint, since no product can live up to a false expectation.

➤ Failure to keep promises – unreliability is akin to LYING.

➤ Not following up on quotes, presentations or demonstrations wastes the buyer's TIME.

These are only a few of the ways to dupe buyers, any one of which can cause them to evaporate. Why not simply keep your mouth shut except to say what has to be said, ears open to hear what has to be heard, and eyes focused on what has to be seen to complete the task of doing the best job for your customer. It would be the easiest route to maintaining an honest reputation.

With the rising price of gasoline and other variable costs, a salesperson wheeling around town is running up a real tab against the expense account these days. To alleviate the strain, careful planning of every sales visit to make it as worthwhile as possible is vital. However, follow-ups are pivotal to reducing costs and improving sales totals. Throwing in a bunch of white lies, cover-ups and alibis for poor planning is a waste of resources and money. Every single one of the points above has at their root a greater problem – lack of sales knowledge.

Rather than provide more reasons for a buyer not to purchase from you, why not learn what is necessary to maintain a high level of performance in your sales job. That way, there would be no temptation to hide ineptitude by using unprofessional techniques that smack of dishonesty.

The cost of untruth is high for both the salesperson and their employer. Reduce the chance of losing customers by exercising common sense in dealings, studying constantly to improve sales techniques, and resisting the temptation to stretch the facts. Integrity is the one trait that salespeople should never lose, for if they do, they can kiss their customer goodbye. So, do you have all the business you can stand?

Oh, I'm sorry.
I thought you
meant what
you said.

SILLY ME!

GIVE 'EM JUST A LITTLE MORE

It sounds like a cliché, "Give a customer a bit more than her or she actually pays for." Why would any business want to do it, though? Giving away even small amounts of sellable product is a cost that builds up against the bottom line. Surely it would be a waste of time, effort and product to do so. Perhaps—but let's not forget that there is more to the bottom line than profits.

What about customer satisfaction? Aren't happy customers what all businesses want? Sure it is. No business wants a bad reputation. In this day of high tech marketing, reaching out to prospective buyers is easier than ever before. Yet, among all the ways of getting the word out, every business must contend with what people say about them after the sale. That's why a bit of oiling is necessary. It helps eliminate squeaks, and even dispels most rattles.

Word-of-mouth advertising is a force easily overlooked because most companies never hear what people say about them. Let's use a generic "restaurant" for an example. It is easy to see when a restaurant is successful, because the parking lot is full during business hours. People who are satisfied with a particular restaurant's food and service tell their friends about the experience. Their friends visit the restaurant, and they in turn tell more friends about the great food and wonderful encounter. Soon, the whole town knows how good this particular restaurant is and—viola—the restaurant is successful! The restaurant didn't have to spend a dime on the media to get this positive advertising. It only had to produce good food and good service.

Likewise, the same restaurant may change something about its food or service, the experience is cheapened in some way, and word-of-mouth advertising causes the death of a once-successful eatery. Every restaurant proprietor fears the "empty parking lot." Some even cause the employees to park prominently out front to give the impression that all is as it once was. Yet, nothing can repair the damage that word-of-mouth advertising did. Somewhere along the way, this restaurant stopped oiling its customers, and I don't mean cutting out the fried foods!

John White, once owner-operator of Spartanburg, South Carolina's famous Beacon Restaurant, was a master over word-of-mouth advertising. He knew how to grease the squeaky wheel. Not only did every plate of food contain more than the customer paid for, but if anyone took the time to give him a compliment, he would give them something extra. Sometimes it would be whole apple pies, other times a scoop of ice cream, once in a while homemade cookies. I know, because I complimented him a lot! Once, my grandmother dropped by to pick up a pound of barbeque hash, and when she got home, the container was not nearly as full as she thought it should have been. She called and complained. Mr. White took her name, address and telephone number, and apologized. Within fifteen minutes, a Beacon employee showed up on her doorstep with three pounds of hash, her money back for the first pound of hash, and a handwritten note from Mr. White asking her to return! To this day, the Beacon Restaurant has carried on the tradition of excellent customer service, as evidenced by their full parking lot.

In short, the best way to keep customers coming back is to make sure they stay happy. If a customer is disgruntled, rectify the situation immediately. Word-of-mouth advertising, both positive and negative, can mean the affluence or destruction of a company. A bit of oiling, something even as simple as a smile of gratitude, may be all it takes to get the customer's tongue a-wagging about how great that company is. Spend a small amount of the advertising budget on oil instead of glitzy media. No amount of advertising money can beat the influence of friends telling friends telling friends telling friends...

NO BLOOPER CLEANING SAFETY

Cleaning personnel are supposed to be trained to recognize potential hazards that may cause injury, or even death, yet I see safety procedures ignored all the time. Occupational Safety and Health Administration (OSHA) would frown on code violations, and levy fines of course, but that doesn't stop unwary or untrained cleaning staff from bending or breaking the rules. In the cleaning industry safety hazards fall into several categories: chemical, biological, equipment, and bloopers (accidents). It is important that cleaning folks are properly trained to avoid procedures that could cause harm, especially since violations open the door to liability lawsuits and disability claims.

The foremost area of training should be on material safety data sheets, required by law to be onsite in commercial/industrial situations where cleaning chemicals are used. These sheets tell exactly what type of protection should be worn for all types of cleaning chemicals. Items such as gloves, goggles, aprons, rubber shoes, etc., are listed as well as what types of chemical combinations to avoid, and emergency medical procedures in case of improper exposure. In all my years working with cleaning staff, the most prevalent infraction remains mixing incompatible cleaning chemicals, namely bleach and ammonia, common cleaners used everywhere (although they shouldn't be). When these two common chemicals are mixed, they form chloramine gas, highly toxic, and well known to cause death. To avoid chemical mistakes, read and follow the recommendations on the SDS!

Next, biological hazards are high on the list of bloopers. For instance, I have personally witnessed janitorial staff members reaching in to a toilet to remove empty deodorant canisters, or picking up spent urinal screens *with their bare hands!* It's almost enough to make me retch just thinking about all those zillions of potentially hazardous germs that got transferred to bare skin. When confronted about such hazardous cleaning habits, I usually hear these words or something similar, "It ain't no big deal. Hands wash off." Tell that to HIV, hepatitis, pinworms, herpes, and uncountable other biological nuisances. Personally, I would prefer all the protection I can get in this line of work.

Finally, equipment bloopers usually send cleaning personnel to the disability shelf. Ladders and stepstools, tools of the trade, are needed to clean above the head things like windows, light fixtures, spider webs in corners, and such. Stacked boxes and rickety chairs do not qualify as replacements for these vital tools. Neither does ignoring the warning label on the next to the last ladder rung concerning weight limits and height limits. I watched a man bust his skull when he fell from atop the highest step of a fourteen-foot-tall A-framed ladder once upon a time. I never want to see anything like it again. One other example pertains to running side-to-side rotary scrubbing machines. These machines are powerful units designed to remove wax from floors with strippers and such. The chemicals used in combination with these machines are slick when applied to virtually any floor surface. Imagine using flat-soled shoes on a surface that is slicker than ice while holding the handle (reins) of a one-horse-power (or larger) rotary machine. Now imagine that machine slamming the operator through sheetrock wall. Yes, I've seen that too.

Preventative maintenance in the cleaning industry is a matter of following material safety recommendations; however, repetitive work begs complacency. Staff training should include frequent reminders to follow safety procedures. There should also be a system in place to handle infractions of these vital safety rules. Just because a janitor has slung a mop for forty years does not mean he or she knows how to stay safe while on the job. In fact, I see more safety errors committed by seasoned cleaning staff than by rank amateurs. Inexperienced cleaning folks pay more attention to details, especially where it concerns their personal safety. Novices read the labels, follow the steps, and listen when I convey warnings, whereas those "in the biz" tend to ignore what I say because they've seen it all and done it all before. To those ignoramuses I state that I believe in a "no blooper" scenario in order to stay safe and happy. Do you?

SOAP IS NOT AN OPERA

Soaps are staple products of the cleaning industry, yet most contractors do not understand how to pick from among the myriad choices on the market. I base this comment on thirty-plus years of experience in janitorial supply sales and service. Lack of knowledge makes contractors susceptible to ridiculous advertising too. Genies, captains, ditsy housewives, and talking bubbles play heavily in this arena. There's a lot of hype and voodoo surrounding the soap industry which needs to be dispelled. This is especially true when it comes to "green" products. Like a soap opera, with constant turmoil as the rule of the plot, regulatory agencies, the Green Movement, and major manufacturers keep the show riveting. To save money and get the job done, cleaning contractors must become savvy buyers; otherwise, precious dollars will be flushed down the toilet. With this in mind, let's begin to dispel the misconceptions.

SOAP MAKING

First, it is important to know a teeny bit of chemistry. Soap is nothing more than a basic reaction between animal fat or vegetable oil and caustic soda, commonly called lye. Mix the two components together and poof, you've made soap. Your great-great-grandmother used to do it at home with lye water made from fireplace ashes and leftover grease from cooking. Soap itself if nothing more than a salt, the result of combining acidic fats or oils with alkalis like caustic. There are many types of salts, table salt being the most familiar; however, we are concerned with salt of a fatty acid – soap.

Creating soap is known as saponification, from the Latin word *sapo,* meaning soap. Modern day soaps are a bit more complex to make, however the chemical reaction is basically the same. We call them detergents these days, but they perform the same basic task as great-great-granny's lye soap – lowering the surface tension of water (more on this later). Detergents have many uses, from synthetic lubricants to disinfectants. We will only concern ourselves with those used in the cleaning industry.

pH SCALE

Now for a bit more chemistry: the pH Scale. This scale measures the strength of an acid (like vinegar or battery acid) and a base (like caustic, an alkali). Here is a simplified version of the scale:

75

Battery Acid		Vinegar	Tallow		Milk	Water	Baking Soda		Ammonia			Lye

← →

0	1	2	3	4	5	6	7	8	9	10	11	12	13	14
ACIDIC						NEUTRAL							BASIC	

What is most important to understand here is that acids and alkalis are not the same – they are opposites – opposites attract and very possibly react. Many problems arise from not grasping this concept. For instance, a marble floor must never be cleaned with acid (i.e., vinegar) because acids react with the limestone in the marble to permanently damage the stone; an acrylic waxed floor must never be cleaned with a base (i.e., household ammonia) because it will strip the acrylic. Taking time to thoroughly comprehend the pH scale is imperative when it comes to purchasing the right detergent for the task (See Figure 1). Both the composition of the surface to be cleaned and the type of cleaning chemical to use must be taken into account to avoid damaging reactions. [When in doubt, a good janitorial supply house should be able to offer assistance. Build a relationship with one you trust.]

Without having to test every cleaning chemical with litmus paper or a meter to determine the pH, there are easier ways to get this information: The Safety Data Sheet (SDS) on all chemicals as required by Occupational Health and Safety Administration (OSHA), the manufacturer's Product Technical Bulletin (tech sheet), the seller of the product, and the internet. Most manufacturers provide both SDSs and Tech Sheets via their websites. Yet another way to determine the compatibility of a detergent with a job type is to READ the product label. I can't say this strongly enough. Labeling contains instructions for use, precautions, and warnings. As a cleaning contractor, all of these sources of product information should be used and stored as a matter of permanent record at the contractor's place of business.

SURFACE TENSION

Now, let's get back to surface tension and how it affects your bottom line. Surface tension is the ability of a liquid to resist external force. Ever seen a paper clip floating on water (see Figure 1)? Surface tension is what keeps it afloat. The same principle makes plain water a relatively poor way to clean a surface of any type. Every surface has tiny pores and blemishes that

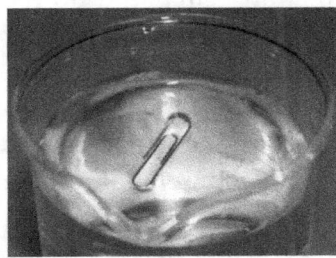

Figure 1

harbor dirt and germs (see Figure 2). The surface tension of water covers over those blemishes much like a skin, which in turn traps the debris in those near-microscopic pockets. The addition of a detergent to water reduces the surface tension so that the cleaning solution will sink into the blemishes, allowing the dirt and germs to float free (see Figure 4). The detergent then buoys and surrounds the dirt and germs so they can't sink back to the surface as easily. We call this increasing the surface's "wettability." This is why you never clean anything with just plain water. A good quality cleaning detergent makes the job go faster – simple as that. One further way to enhance the cleaning ability of any water-based detergent or soap is to dilute them in warm water. The surface tension of warm water is less than cold water, thus the ability to get in tinier pores is improved, therefore freeing more dirt and germs. Axiom: increasing the ability to clean a surface reduces labor and chemical costs dramatically.

The next consideration toward saving money on cleaners is to use commercial quality detergents as opposed to consumer brands designed for home use. Homeowners are not generally as knowledgeable as professional cleaning contractors when it comes to using detergents; thus, household products are not normally as strong as their commercial counterparts. After all, cleaning contractors are supposed to be bonded, insured, and competent in the use of stouter commercial detergents. [Example: while a full 8-ounce cup of the name brand household pine cleaner is required in a gallon of water, many commercial equivalents can be diluted as much as an ounce per gallon.] Overuse not only increases chemical costs, but also the possibility of causing damage to both people and surfaces. While it is very important to use commercial cleaners to keep costs down, it is equally important to obtain proper training in their use.

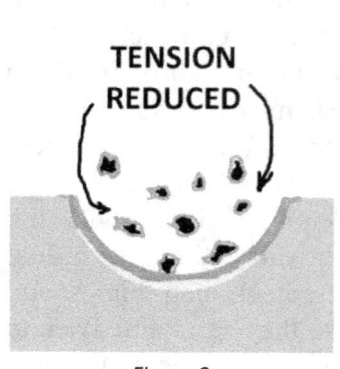

TENSION REDUCED

Figure 2

Richard C. Meehan, Jr.

GOING GREEN

Now, here comes the voodoo. Most manufacturers would like you to think that they have the finest, "greenest," most concentrated quality cleaning chemicals on the market today. While constant research is being done to make better, "greener" detergents, that doesn't mean there is much progress. The Green Movement, supposedly geared toward making the world more environmentally conscious, is actually driving up manufacturing costs by lobbying for more stringent rules and regulations over cleaning products and procedures. OSHA complies without hesitation because it means more fines, fees, licenses, and restrictions that fill government coffers with money. Biodegradability is a buzz word of the Greenies. The fact is, nearly all water-based cleaning detergents are biodegradable and always have been. When they breakdown in nature they become mostly fertilizer (various salts, remember). Simply put, they rot. Most cleaning detergents only become hazardous once they are contaminated with dirt, grease, germs, and other more hazardous materials.

DETERGENT CONCENTRATES

Since "going green" means more expense for everyone, it is important that cleaning contractors learn how to stretch their detergent dollars. The biggest savings will come from purchasing quality concentrates in bulk. Water, commonly known as "the universal solvent," is a key ingredient, and a cost, in the making of detergents. While some water must be present, more water is an extra cost – purified water is not free. Production of concentrated detergents costs less than making those with low or nonexistent dilution rates, mainly because of packaging labor and materials. The increased labor of putting detergents in quart bottles versus fifty-five gallon drums is astronomical. It takes ten times longer to pour a case of a dozen quarts as it does to pour fifty-five gallons into a drum. Oh, but what about automation? Sure, expensive filling machines can cut costs over time for packaging zillions of gallons. Not all manufacturers of quality detergents are large enough to support them though. Let's look at some real figures:

EXAMPLE: A gallon of a quality concentrated degreaser currently runs about $13, having a proven dilution ratio that works for the job at the rate of 1part degreaser to 64 parts water. A gallon of "use-as-is" degreaser costs around $8 and will do the job too. How much is the real cost per square foot for each product? Given: a gallon of liquid detergent covers about 1200 square feet.

A. The Concentrate: 1/64 = .016 dilution ratio. Multiplying $13 x .016 = $0.21 per gallon. This makes the real cost of degreasing 1200 square feet a mere 21 cents!

B. The Use-As-Is: 1/1 = 1 dilution ratio. Multiplying $8 x 1 = $8 per gallon. This makes the real cost of degreasing 1200 square feet a whopping $8!

From the example we can see that the actual cost of degreasing 1200 square feet with the proven concentrated degreaser, even though we pay dramatically more, is by far the most economical product to use! This same method of calculation can be used to determine the real costs involved with every type of detergent. A final tip: avoid buying fancy packages, especially dilution control bottles and premeasured pods. Often the packaging costs more than the actual detergent. Buy in bulk.

DILUTION CONTROL

Once the chemical costs have been calculated and the best product for the job is chosen, it comes down to proper training of the end user to insure that we eliminate the biggest drain on our investment – waste. This brings us to dilution control. Nearly any container

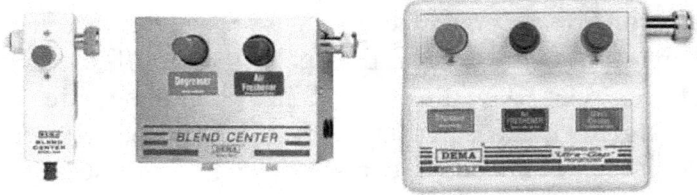

Figure 5 – Push Button Blend Centers

Images courtesy of DEMA Engineering (www.demaeng.com)

can be filled using exact ratios, thus removing the possibility of human error and waste. As long as the proper ratio for the job is achieved, it doesn't matter how simple or complex the dilution method. Use of a measuring cup is about as easy as it gets. Buy one. Make copious notes on the dilution ratios that work best with each detergent in your cleaning arsenal.

If you are a larger contractor and are still allowing

your employees to use the glug-glug method of dilution control, it would be extremely prudent to obtain a proportioning system. Also known as chemical proportioners, blend centers, dispensing systems, and dilution control stations, these devices meter specified amounts of detergent into water automatically (see Figure 5). These systems come in many configurations and range from about $80 to $600. Find a proportioning system that handles all of the cleaning detergents you use no matter what the final expense in equipment. Equipment costs are minimal when compared to detergent waste. The investment will be recouped very quickly.

As bulk chemicals have a lower cost per gallon, it behooves us to buy in as large a container as we can afford. For a contract cleaning service, that means a bare minimum size of five gallon pails of the best concentrates we can find. Since the shelf life on detergents is measured in years (if in a properly sealed container), and since contract cleaning services use these products every day, I have always recommended purchasing in thirty or fifty-five gallon drums. Dispensing into smaller containers, properly diluted, cuts detergent costs as far as they can go. Just think, if an employee uses three glugs from the jug of disinfectant, that's a bare minimum of ten ounces. If that same employee only puts two gallons of water in the mop bucket, that's a ratio of five ounces per gallon. If the detergent calls for one ounce per gallon of water, that employee just quintupled the detergent cost for the job! Consider this: your company currently buys 180 gallons of neutral cleaner each year. The glug-glug method causes a minimum of one-fifth of the 180 gallons to go down the drain. That's 180/5 = 36 gallons wasted. The detergent cost is $6.90 per gallon, so 36 x 6.90 = $248.40. Since dilution control units for drums only run about $100, you tell me, is it worth it to control waste?

DETERGENT QUALITY

Our next consideration is quality of the detergents used. If a detergent does not help get the job done in a timely fashion with a reasonable amount of labor, get another detergent that does. Once the proper type of detergent is picked for the job, following instructions on the label will establish the quality. For instance, general damp mopping of waxed floors calls for a neutral cleaner; your brand of neutral cleaner states to pour three ounces in a gallon of warm water to damp mop a waxed floor. Further, the detergent label says to apply liberally with a mop and allow five minutes to soak, and then sop up. Does it work? If so, purchase more; otherwise, find another brand. The worst case scenario: your cleaning crew of three (hourly wage of $7.25) was slated to spend six hours mopping the gym floor at a church. Your detergent indicated that you would use five gallons (cost of $6.90 per gallon) and be able to mop once. Instead, it took nine gallons, plus fourteen hours of labor. That's 14 – 6 = 8 x 3 = 24 hours of extra time, 24 x 7.25 = $174 extra labor, and 9 – 5 = 4 x 6.90 = $27.60 extra detergent for a total extra cost of $201.60. There goes the profit!

The point is you get what you pay for. Buy quality

to save money. This does not mean you have to buy name brand detergents either. There are many smaller manufactures making quality products too. Do the research. Run the tests. Keep the notes. Find the products that work best for your cleaning team!

We've covered much territory in the realm of cleaning chemicals, mainly geared toward how to choose cost efficient, quality detergents to help reduce cleaning costs. Along the way we learned why detergents are used, why cheap is not actually cost conscious, why dilution control is imperative, and why becoming knowledgeable about basic chemistry as it pertains to detergents will help us exorcise the voodoo surrounding soap making. The "soap opera" of changing rules and regulations perpetuated by the Green Movement, manufacturers, and the feds does not have to break our contract cleaning companies. We may have to take into account all the directives pushing our costs higher, but at least now we can filter out much of the hype so we can get down to the business of making a profit through educated detergent purchasing.

Richard C. Meehan, Jr.

BLEACH AND AMMONIA DON'T MIX

Bleach and ammonia have been prime chemicals used by the cleaning industry since the Industrial Revolution. They're cheap, at least in their undiluted form. Cheap does not mean clean however. Sure, both chemicals are stout and will clean stuff, but are they a good way to cut cleaning costs? Let's look at some of the pros and cons:

CONS:

1. Bleach and ammonia are dangerous and hazardous. Thinking of "going green?" Forget it with these chemicals. Both are heavy disinfectants used in water purification and waste treatment facilities. They eliminate creatures from the water supply – including fish.
2. These chemicals contain no detergents, so improving the wettability of the mopping solution is limited. Dirt

simply falls back to the surface even as you mop. (See article, "Soap is Not an Opera" for more information.)

3. They both burn skin and damage incompatible surfaces like waxed floors.
4. Neither is very dilutable for cleaning purposes, which means greater chemical costs.
5. There are certainly a few surfaces that respond well to bleach or ammonia, but I can't think of any. Both chemicals put wear and tear on most types of surfaces.
6. The two products accidently mixed together will give off toxic chloramine fumes and kill you.

PROS:

1. Bleach takes out some stains from some surfaces, mainly fabrics.
2. Ammonia makes an okay glass cleaner if you can stand the smell.

By employing Benjamin Franklin's method of decision-making, we see that the cons outweigh the pros. Don't use these chemicals to replace detergent cleaners unless you want to pay more to get less cleaning done, plus add to your liability on the job.

Richard C. Meehan, Jr.

THE WET MOP HANDLE DISSECTED

Mops and mop handles are the staple tools of the contract cleaning industry, yet many janitorial and maid folks do not know how to choose the right combination for a job. Strangely enough, as with most tools and equipment, the right mop can mean the difference between mediocre and great performance. For this article I will use the terms for "mops" and "mop handles" fairly interchangeably to reduce confusion and verbiage. After all, it's hard to use a mop head without a mop handle. Suffice it to say that getting the right combo can mean the difference between profitability and breakeven, backache and heartache.

Ergonomics is a big word that became trendy in the 1980s. I was enamored with the backless secretary chairs that came out. Hook your knees under the stirrup and sit comfortably straight for typing at a desk. What was forgotten in the design was the need to rest periodically – slouch in your chair. You simply couldn't, and forget extricating your legs in a hurry. You'd end up tumbling in the floor with the chair on top. That's the way it is with incorrect mops for the task too. Ergonomics actually translates into the ability to work longer with less strain. A properly matched mop-to-job ratio allows janitorial staff to work more efficiently without getting hurt.

Let's break down the moving parts. A mop consists of a handle and a head. When choosing the right combo, several factors must be considered:

- Length – handles come in a variety from 54 to 64 inches.
- Width – handle frames come in widths of 6 to 7 inches.
- Diameter – handle diameter ranges from 1 to 1.25 inches.
- Weight – handles combined with heads can top out at about 5 dry pounds.
- Style – handle and head styles directly affect ergonomics and efficiency.
- The Person – the size and strength of the person using the mop determines the style of handle and mop head, not the job size.

While we have always been told that bigger is better, not so with mops. A custom fit is far more important than size. If you wear out the janitor, work stops; therefore, it is always best to fit the mopping equipment to the person.

Richard C. Meehan, Jr.

Let's begin a custom fit by considering handle length. The rule of thumb is this: if the person is 5.5 feet or less in height, choose a handle of less the 60 inches long; if the person is greater than 5.5 feet tall, choose a handle longer than 60 inches. When the mop hits the floor, as shown in the picture at right, there should be approximately a 45-degree angle formed by the handle, the floor, and the janitor's body. Coupled with slightly bent knees this is a balanced stance, ergonomically sound.

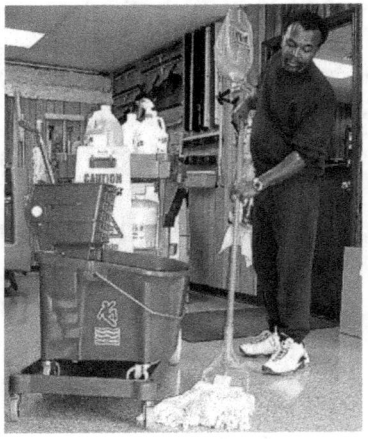

Next, the size of the mop head itself is a weight issue. While my next article will discuss the materials used to make mops, in general it

Alexander Nash

is a good idea to use a lighter mop head for a smaller person and conversely a heavier mop head for a larger person. A 12-ounce rayon mop head together with a 54" tall handle only weighs about 1.5-pounds dry. Once wet, the weight increases to about 2 pounds. A 32-ounce cotton mop head together with a 64" tall handle weighs about 3 pounds dry and 7 pounds wet. Placing a 7-pound combo in a 98-pound lady's hands would be like hanging that much lead weight from her neck at the start of the job. By the time she finished mopping 1000 square feet, every muscle in her body would ache. Remember that she not only has to push the mop, but rinse and wring it out constantly in the mop bucket. Lifting, pulling, tugging – one can only get used to so much exercise. Lighten the load to 2 pounds and get twice the work done in less time before she poops out.

Handle thickness can cause issues too. The same small lady most likely has hands to match her stature, so a thick handle would mean that her grip would have to be stronger to control the extra weight. To prevent undue strain from an improper grip, tennis players have their racquets customized. The same principle should be applied to a mop handle. A proper diameter relieves pressure in the hands so a person may work longer with less fatigue.

The width of the mop frame at the end of the handle determines the size of mop head that will work well for that handle. If the frame is 5 inches wide and the mop head is 8 inches, there's going to be some cramming going on. Generally, the width of the frame needs to be slightly wider than the mop head for easy

Straight Bar	Swing-away Bar	Claw Gripper	Threaded Post

installation and removal. This is just another little time factor that adds up toward less getting done on the job.

Another time eater is the ability (or lack thereof)

to remove an old mop head quickly and easily. Handles are offered with a variety of framework choices: straight bar, swing-away bar, claw gripper, and threaded post.

The straight bar handle is the least expensive monetarily but most expensive time-wise. A string mop will most likely have to be cut away from the straight bar, while all other handle types allow for easy frame access. In order of speedy head replacement, the threaded post is quickest followed by the claw gripper, swing-away bar, with the straight bar in last place.

Consider the human factor too. A big mop is daunting to a small person; a small mop is frustrating to a large person. If a janitor is not very conscientious on the job, meaning he or she tends toward laziness, then choosing an incorrect mop may be a way of going slower, getting less done in the time allotted, or simply becoming fatigued faster so as to take a longer break. On the opposite end of the spectrum, someone wanting to get done quickly would be quite upset using a 6-inch-wide mop on a large area. They may never get done with the job! So remember, mop size must be matched to the person and the purpose, not the overall job size.

Get a handle on job costs by controlling the ergonomics behind simple mopping equipment. Prevent injury and undue fatigue by matching the right length, width, weight, diameter, and style of handle to the person slinging the mop. Next time I'll address how to choose the right mop head for the job, but for now, access your handle situation and be prepared for the "wow" when the correct handle is put to use.

BECOME THE BRAND

The black hat consideration

A great number of salespeople are barely more than common hucksters, figments of their sales manager's desires for greater sales and profits. It is a shame too, since all of them could improve vastly in a matter of seconds if only they had a  slight change of heart. All they have to do is become the brand. This is the most basic rule of good salesmanship, not a cosmic secret. Branding, or creating name recognition for a product or service, is the function of salespeople, and especially business owners, yet few understand the concept. Said best by Hawk, the bad guy in the black hat on John Wayne's western movie *Rooster Cogburn*, "You take my money, you wear my brand!" This sentiment is, of course, mirrored by every company in America, albeit not as sinisterly put. Salespeople are needed for the generation of profits, so companies endeavor to hire those who are willing to become the "brand." Devotion is expected and deserved in return for the paycheck, but rarely given. Few salespeople actually believe that devotion to the "brand" is necessary; therefore, they fail to meet sales expectations.

Good salespeople want their customers to remember what they represent. For me, I experience a thrill when a customer says, "Here comes the Marko Man!" Marko Janitorial Supply is my company name, my brand of cleaning products, and my livelihood. I take pride in it. When customers see me, I want them to remember I am more than just a nice guy in a suit. I want them to remember I represent a professional brand name worth having on their supply closet shelf!

Sage branding advice

Branding is something Roy C. Getz, chairman of the Ohio Restaurant Association and former Senior Vice President of Marketing for Denny's Restaurants, knows a lot about. He believes, "A clearly defined brand position is critical for ongoing success. We must develop our advertising and merchandising in such a way as to leverage our brand's points of difference. Showing how we

Roy C. Getz, President of Top Notch Restaurant Group

are different and better leads to ongoing business growth, the whole reason for branding."

Wasted branding bucks

Most companies spend advertising dollars for little do-lollies like logo business cards, logo pens, logo ball caps, logo T-shirts, logo coffee mugs and other logo sundries. For a while my company offered magnetic signs which could easily be applied to car doors and removed as needed. Do you think a single one of our salespeople would use them besides myself as sales manager? No! They were too embarrassed to put them on their cars. We had logo caps and shirts at one time too. Do you think a single one of our salespeople would wear them besides myself as sales manager? No! They were too important to wear anything with a logo. When salespeople are not proud enough of what they represent to take advantage of expensive branding tools at their disposal, do you think they will make it? NO!

I sell toilet paper, hand towels, mop buckets, floor finishes, disinfectants, and all sorts of cleaning products. What my customers remember upon seeing me is that I sell toilet paper. So be it! As long as they remember my brand and put my toilet tissue on their holder, I have succeeded as a salesperson. I put up with the jokes because every chuckle is yet another branding technique. "Hey, do you sell John Wayne toilet tissue? You know, the kind that's rough and tough and don't take !2#1!&%! from nobody?" Nope. I don't. I leave that to my competition, pardner;

however, if you want something worth using, buy it from me. You'll find my company logo on every box just to remind you of where to come for skid paper.

My point is this: it doesn't matter what you sell but how you represent it. Do yourself and your company a favor and earn your keep by understanding how important it is to talk up the brand. This one simple change in the manner of a sales call will dramatically increase sales over time. It is a fundamental shift in thought. I am the Marko Man. Marko stands for quality products, excellent personalized service, and competitive pricing. What does your brand stand for? If you can't state the answer in a single short sentence, you've already failed before you get started selling. Do your company a favor and don't waste branding bucks. Embrace the brand to improve sales.

Wear the hat!

It is lack of devotion that breaks a brand. The top complaint I hear from defunct salespeople is, "They [the company] didn't give me what they said they would." My joiner is, "Did you give them all you said you would?" By that I mean, "Did you become the brand for them?" After all, salespeople are most times the only faces seen of a company by the customer.

Rick Meehan
Author

They are the company in the minds of their clientele. That's why devotion is so important, to make believers out of customers. If a salesperson does not believe in the products he or she represents, how would anyone else be able to? Just as the bad guy always wears black - a branding technique used by writers and promoters of movie and television Westerns - a salesperson should don the garb of his or her brand. Wear the hat!

Richard C. Meehan, Jr.

THE MAGIC VACUUM

Once upon a time, in the dark ages of the nineteen-eighties, I sold the latest, greatest, newfangled vacuum cleaner to a little old maid at a church. She loved the machine. It got under the pews, it cleaned the hallways thoroughly, and the preacher was happy with the sparkling shag carpet in his plush office. I made regular visits to check the stock of towels, toilet tissue, hand soap, and other sundries, so I saw the maid often. The maid loved the vacuum because it made her work easier. It was a good sale for a good reason.

However, not all tales have a silver lining. Sometimes it is necessary to check for worn or frayed threads. As a sales representative who wanted my customers to be happy, and think of me as their go-to person for cleaning supplies and information, I always ask about how the products I have sold are doing. I made my regular visit to the maid one morning and discovered that she was very unhappy with her vacuum.

She had only used the vacuum for three weeks,

and already the machine simply would not pick up any dirt. It ran. The brush turned. When the machine was running, dirt flew out from underneath instead of being picked up. This was not right. She wanted satisfaction!

I thought and thought. Finally, I opened the canvas vacuum bag to see whether the inner paper filter bag was in place, when what to my eyes did appear – a completely jam-packed paper filter bag. It was so full of sand, grit, debris, and dust, from top to bottom, that not one more spec would be able to enter it!

"Here's the problem," I sagely exclaimed. "The bag's full!"

She looked at me with a vacant expression. "What bag?"

"The disposable paper filter bag," said I. There was no change in her face. She really didn't know what I was saying, so I gently asked, "Where did you think the dirt goes?"

The little maid rolled her eyes and said, "Why, it's being vacuumed up of course! That's the way a vacuum should work. It picks up the dirt and gets rid of it."

Trying not to marvel, I placed a spare vacuum bag in the unit, careful to make sure she watched me and understood what had to be done. I even made her take the full bag and put it in the trash so she knew the dirt was being "gotten rid of." Her vacuum now worked again – like magic. All was well. End of story. Almost.

You see, I never forgot that experience. I had made a huge assumption. I thought that everyone understood how a vacuum cleaner worked. This maid was not a stupid person. I simply had missed showing her a crucial part of operating her new machine. It was my fault that the machine stopped removing dirt from her floors!

Moral of the story: We are all representatives in one way or another. We represent ourselves to others each day by simply walking out our own doors, if for no other reason. I have made my livelihood explaining all kinds of cleaning systems to all kinds of people. When I fail to make a point, it is MY FAULT. When I fail to make a sale, it is MY FAULT. When I lose a customer to a competitor, it is MY FAULT. As an aspiring contractor in the World of Clean, if you fail, it is YOUR FAULT.

Now, go out armed with what you have begun to learn here and make yourself an expert in the cleaning industry. If you follow some of what we have discussed and learn everything you can about your business, you will succeed! *There are no magic vacuums.* Product knowledge, sales knowledge, procedure knowledge, business knowledge, and elbow grease will ward off defeat and make you a magician in the World of Clean!

APPENDIX

DETERGENT DILUTION RATIO CHART

RATIO	OUNCES OF DETERGENT	OUNCES OF WATER
1:1	128	128
2:1	64	128
3:1	42.7	128
4:1	32	128
5:1	25.6	128
6:1	21.4	128
7:1	18.3	128
8:1	16	128
9:1	14.2	128
10:1	12.8	128
16:1	8	128
20:1	6.4	128
30:1	4.3	128
40:1	3.2	128
50:1	2.6	128
64:1	2	128

Richard C. Meehan, Jr.

DETERGENT DILUTION RATIO CHART (p.2)		
100:1	1.3	128
128:1	1	128
175:1	.75	128
256:1	.50	128
512:1	.25	128
600:1	.22	128
800:1	.16	128
1000:1	.13	128

For any ratio calculation, divide 128 ounces by the detergent part, usually the larger number of the ratio (Example: 50:1 means 128/50 = 2.6 ounces).

ABOUT THE AUTHOR

I was born in Charlotte, North Carolina on July 18, 1960. In 1963, my family moved to Spartanburg, South Carolina where my father went to work as a chemist for a textile detergent manufacturer. Richard Sr., Pop, founded Marko Chemical, Inc. in 1968, and proceeded to build the company into a leading supplier of quality janitorial products. The foundation of Pop's business was his personally formulated Marko brand cleaning detergent line, quality soaps for all types of tough jobs.

From the beginning, I was known as the S.O.B.

(son-of-boss), a position I still hold. Although Pop passed away in 1991, my mother, Ann B. Meehan still runs the show. Pop started me off right, mowing the grass with a sling blade. I was eight. My expertise comes from growing with the biz. I can now speak intelligently on a variety of subjects surrounding the World of Clean.

Nothing much happened while I was growing up unless you consider my hands-on experience manufacturing and packaging detergents every summer vacation from the time I was knee high to a grasshopper. I almost shortened my legs with that sling blade, but the grasshopper got away.

As I grew older, manual labor became an after school pastime. Pop was all for teaching a good work ethic. My mistake came when I learned to type, not "keyboard," but real live typing on an authentic Royal manual typewriter at Spartanburg High School. That's when my mother got a grip on me. She found out that I was really good at processing sextuplicate forms, and erasing errors on all carbon copies of the same, as necessary, every day after band practice. Eventually she discovered that I could crank the adding machine to figure salesmen's commissions to the penny.

Then I went off to Wofford College, all the way across town, in 1978. That's where I learned about business and got my B.A. in Economics. On my graduation day, Pop shook my hand, said "congratulations" and told me that I would start work as a salesman on Monday morning at 8:00 A.M. sharp. I knew nothing about selling anything to anyone, but protestations never worked in my family. My mantra became, "Come rain nor shine nor sleet nor snow, the Marko Man is always on the go," and *go* I did for fifteen years. After Pop died it was back to working at the plant where a small portion of my job was sales manager.

From 1991, my position grew until all hats were worn, from business writer to IT specialist, from webmaster to ecommerce designer, from shipping clerk to delivery guy, from accountant to insurance agent, from equipment repairman to demonstrator, from Material Safety Data writer to training specialist – you name it, I got 'er done. That's the way a family owned and operated business is. You do whatever it takes to make it work. There's nothing peachy about it and every penny of salary is earned.

I have spent my life garnering industry knowledge through blood, sweat, tears, and hands on, rolled-sleeve, janitorial work. With a tongue-in-cheek style, I will address the myths, legends, truths, and fiction surrounding a quirky industry where word-of-mouth advertising can make or break a contract cleaning company overnight. Interwoven with the facts and figures, tips and tricks, admonishments and warnings will be tales of real life situations with names changed to protect the innocent. Running a cleaning company is not for the faint of heart, so prepare yourself for the gritty, yet rewarding, occupation of improving the World of Clean.